To Jessica ~
Have fun with this!
Andy Sullivan

SEWING *with* LEATHER *and* SUEDE

SEWING with LEATHER and SUEDE

A HOME SEWER'S GUIDE

TIPS
TECHNIQUES
INSPIRATION

SANDY SCRIVANO

LARK BOOKS
ASHEVILLE, NORTH CAROLINA

EDITOR
Carol Parks

ART DIRECTOR
Chris Bryant

PHOTOGRAPHY
Evan Bracken

ILLUSTRATIONS
Bernie Wolf

PRODUCTION ASSISTANT
Hannes Charen

Library of Congress Cataloging-in-Publication Data

Scrivano, Sandy.
    Sewing with leather and suede : a home sewer's guide : tips,
techniques, inspirations / by Sandy Scrivano—1st ed.
      p.   cm.
    Includes index.
    ISBN 1-57990-051-8 (hard)
    1. Leather garments. 2. Sewing. I. Title
TT524.S39 1998
646'. 1—dc21   98–22032
                                      CIP

10 9 8 7 6 5 4 3 2 1

First Edition

Published by Lark Books
50 College St.
Asheville, NC 28801, USA

© 1998, Sandy Scrivano

Distributed by Random House, Inc., in the United States, Canada,
the United Kingdom, Europe,and Asia

Distributed in Australia by Capricorn Link (Australia) Pty Ltd.,
P.O. Box 6651, Baulkham Hills Business Centre, NSW 2153, Australia

Distributed in New Zealand by Tandem Press Ltd.,
2 Rugby Rd., Birkenhead, Auckland, New Zealand

Printed in Hong Kong

ISBN 1-57990-051-8

Contents

Introduction

Chapter 1: **How Leather is Made** 8

Chapter 2: **Learning about Leather** 16

Chapter 3: **Tools and Equipment** 32

Chapter 4: **Special Techniques for Leather and Suede** 45

Chapter 5: **Projects to Get You Started** 60

Chapter 6: **Techniques for Garmentmaking** 80

Chapter 7: **Making a Garment** 90

Chapter 8: **Accents and Embellishments** 102

Chapter 9: **Care and Cleaning** 113

Glossary 120

Patterns and Credits 124

Sources 126

Index 127

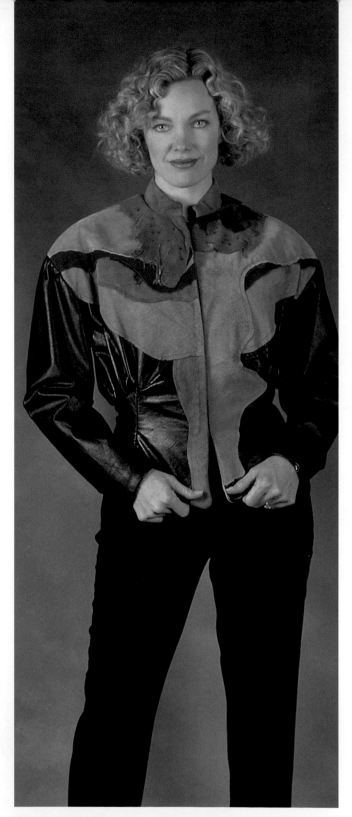

The author's first attempt at sewing with leather and suede resulted in a prize-winning jacket—and this book.

Introduction

A NUMBER OF YEARS AGO I signed up on a whim to take a class on making a leather jacket. The garment I made was black leather with contrasting smooth and sueded leather in shades of rose, lavender, and teal. The zipper was hand picked; the jacket was lined with silk. With a great deal of help from my teacher I turned out a terrific jacket. In fact, it won a first place at the California State Fair.

One day, long afterward, I looked at the jacket and realized I had used the wrong side of the leather on one overlay piece. I also noticed that a few design changes would have simplified the assembly process. It was pretty clear that I needed to expand my education and I started looking for current publications about sewing suede and leather on a home sewing machine. I found piecemeal information, some of it conflicting or outdated, but I did not find a good basic book for my reference library. Filling that need inspired me to write this book.

As home sewers, you and I have the ability to produce high quality garments and accessories at reasonable cost, with a wide range of leather and suede from which to choose. This book addresses the questions of how to select projects, appropriate materials, equipment and supplies, and the procedures for sewing your projects. Sample projects are suggested. A section on care, cleaning, and storage of skins, hides, and garments has been included. The glossary of terminology will make you more knowledgeable, and the garments are meant to inspire you. The more you learn about leather and suede, the more you can appreciate its unique qualities.

About three months before this manuscript was due I had a dream. In it I tried to deliver, in lecture form, all I know about working with leather and suede. As I spoke, one thing after another interrupted or blocked the presentation, and soon the time was gone. I woke with a start and realized the connection with my daytime self. Try as I might, it is impossible to include every iota of information in this book. Do know that it has been well researched to give you, the reader, the best chance at successfully completing garments of leather and suede with your home sewing machine. Several options are given for each construction and finishing technique and plenty of design ideas are shown.

Several people deserve credit for teaching and encouraging me. To Lois Ericson, my adopted Mom, I give respect, gratitude, and admiration. To Diane Ericson, my adopted sister, I give the same. Their generosity has no limit. Many of the techniques I learned from them have been adapted for leather. Marcy Tilton has likewise shared with astonishing openness. Marie Maschmeyer has trained me well. Finally, thanks to Linda Wakefield, my first leather instructor. I sincerely appreciate the introduction. These folks have given me a framework for my creative self.

Additional thanks to Libra Leather, New York, for lending us skins and hides for photography. Kathleen Fasnella discussed washability and interfacing issues with me. Julia Duran also contributed comments about washability Charles Myers, of the Leather Industries of America, gave generously of his time and granted permission to use material from their publication in order to establish standard definitions. The Sewing Emporium in Chula Vista, California, provided supplies.

Thanks to my dear friends Lois Ericson, Diane Ericson, Marcy Tilton, and Nancy Cornelius for sharing their superb designs.

Gale Grigg Hazen and Marcy Tilton generously educated me about the process of writing a book. These are incredible women!

Robert Borg, the chemist who developed Barge Cement 20 years ago, patiently explained the product. Diamond Educational Productions sent a video for me to view that discussed the leather industry in America.

Special thanks to my editor, Carol Parks, at Lark Books for taking a chance with me on this project. It must be a scary thing to work with a new author. I appreciate her courage. Thanks, also, to the other members of the Lark staff who contributed valuable talent and insight. Wow!

Finally, thanks to my family. Each member is truly remarkable!

Soft pigsuede is a good choice for this skirt and matching tie belt. An asymmetric hemline creates interest and the elasticized waist is most comfortable to wear. See pattern information, page 124.

CHAPTER 1

How Leather is Made

Animal skins are the original garment fabrics. Primitive man used skins and fur in a variety of ways to protect against the elements. Egyptian stone carvings five thousand years old show tanners at work. Greeks traded in leather 500 B.C. When the Pilgrims arrived in America, they found Indians making and using leather for clothing and shelter. Today leather is used to make garments of extraordinary design and great durability.

Luxurious beauty is not the only attribute of leather. Along with paper, textiles, sheet rubber and some plastics, it is classed as a flexible sheet material. A cross section reveals the structure that gives leather its unique qualities. The top, or grain, layer and the flesh side, surround an inner corium. Together these layers form a flexible sheet whose basic constituent is collagen. These collagen fibers are intertwined to form long helices, producing a material that is strong and flexible, resistant to abrasion and puncture, and which has the capacity to both absorb and transmit moisture. It insulates and breathes. These are wonderful qualities for garments!

Simply speaking, leather is preserved animal skin with or without its hair or fur. The process of *preservation*, or *tanning*, was originally accomplished by soaking the skins or hides in a solution containing the bark and leaves of certain trees and plants. This process is referred to as *vegetable tanning*, still a viable procedure. A variation of this ancient method is in use today.

Vegetable-tanned leather tends to be stiff and rigid. It is suitable for bags, shoes, western-style items, and industry. The hand and weight of vegetable-tanned leather is usually too heavy and stiff for garments.

American Indians developed another tanning procedure, utilizing the brain of the animal and greasy smoke to produce the soft buckskins used for clothing. *Brain-tanning* is used only for deerskin. While this process creates soft, pliable garment leather, it is limited to the one kind of animal hide.

The cognac-colored pigskin has been vegetable tanned. Vegetable tanning yields leather with a stiffer hand than does mineral or chrome tanning, and such leather is often unsuitable for garment construction. The blue split cow has been sueded on both sides. Split cow is often used for chaps.

This Italian cowhide is finished for use in upholstery. Upholstery leather is processed as whole hides that yield a large usable area. They are often three or more ounces in weight, too heavy for use with a home sewing machine.

Both sides of this Italian calf have been suede finished. This treatment is common for thick hides that are split into several usable layers. Either side of the skin may be used as the "right" side.

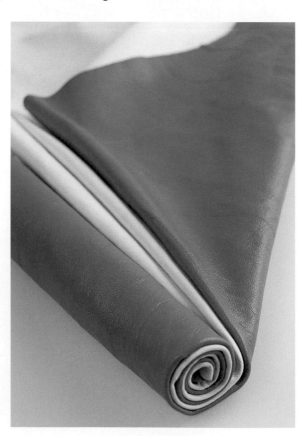

Italian lambskin (green) and calf (bone) are finished with a similar weight and hand. In its natural state, calf is heavier than lamb. This piece has been split.

The Tanning Process

Tanning is a multi-step process that begins with *curing*. A skin or hide is first treated to prevent putrefaction. It is then soaked to restore moisture and to add wetting agents and disinfectants. Next, *unhairing* with chemical depilatories destroys the hair or hair root to free it from the hide. Unhairing loosens the epidermis covering the grain without destroying the collagen. *Bating* removes the unhairing chemicals and non-leather-making substances. The final pre-tanning step is *pickling*, which creates an acid environment for the tanning procedures that follow. At this stage skins and hides are preserved and can be kept in storage for tanning.

Tanning is the process by which skins and hides are converted into stable, non-putrescible material. The most common tanning procedure used to produce garment leathers is *chrome tanning*. Chromium salts are combined with other chemicals to produce chromium sulfate. Skins or hides are soaked in a solution of brine and chromium sulfate. Chrome changes the color of the hide to a blue-green, and a hide at this stage is referred to as *blue*, or *in the blue*. Chrome tanning makes leather more resistant to water by pulling the fibers closer together (remember those intertwined helices).

The next set of procedures prepares the leather for further processing. *Wringing* removes excess moisture, after which the leather is *sorted* according to thickness before splitting. Trimming and siding prepare the hides for splitting and shaving. Oddly shaped areas are trimmed off. Large hides, such as cow, are split from head to tail along the backbone. The resulting pieces are now referred to as *side leather* or *sides. Splitting* adjusts the thickness of the hide by machine. A hide is fed through the machine, grain side up, yielding a grain layer relatively even in thickness. The remaining layer is called a *split*. Lacking grain, it is valuable for making sueded types of leather; however, not all suede is produced from split hides. This will be discussed later. Shaving is done on the grain portion to more precisely level the hide and open the fiber structure to better accept subsequent chemical processing.

Retanning is a second tannage that imparts specific characteristics to the leather depending on the agent or agents used. Vegetable extracts stiffen the hand of chrome-tanned leather as well as reduce variation in character throughout a hide. Syntans (synthetic tanning agents) are used to produce softer leathers. They reduce the intensity of the blue-green color resulting from the chrome tanning and have an evening effect on aniline dyes.

"Nubuck" refers to the finishing process wherein the top grain is lightly buffed to produce a finely napped surface that is smoother than suede. A nubuck finish can be applied to various animal skins or hides; this example is cowhide.

Specialty dyes and finishes change the character of a skin or hide. These samples of lamb and pig have been embossed with pattern or distressed to give a weathered look. Home sewers can add pattern by painting or stenciling.

Lambsuede is the premier garment suede. Its lightweight character and superior drape make it ideal for dressmaker applications like blouses, shirts, and softly flowing skirts.

These lambskins have a mirrorlike patent leather finish. Although it is still flexible, patent leather has less drape than leather finished in other ways, but its water-repellent character makes it a good choice for rainwear.

Mineral retanning agents are used to produce leather with a soft hand or white color. It is commonplace to combine different retanning agents to produce specific qualities.

Leather is colored with pigment or aniline dyes. In pigment dyeing, the surface is coated with pigments or other opaque materials. The surface of the leather is masked somewhat or entirely. This method is sometimes used to cover imperfections in a hide. Aniline dyes are transparent dyes that allow the natural characteristics of the leather to show through, an effect similar to that of using stain on wood. Aniline-dyed leather is usually given a protective coating. It is common to combine dye types and finishes.

Fatliquoring is the addition of oil and fatty substances to the leather. This step increases pliability and tensile strength, and influences the final hand of the leather. *Setting* out smooths and stretches the hide, and removes excess moisture. *Drying* removes all but residual moisture.

Conditioning, sometimes called *wetting back*, introduces controlled amounts of moisture as the first step in final tempering. Conditioning provides lubrication during staking. *Staking* and *dry milling* mechanically soften the leather. In staking, rapidly oscillating pins pound the hide on both sides as a conveyor belt moves it along. In dry milling, the leather is tumbled in drums to accomplish the same thing. This latter method is usually used on garment-weight leathers.

Buffing is a mechanical sanding of the grain surface to eliminate some of the surface blemishes. Leathers that are not buffed are referred to as full grain.

In *finishing*, a film is applied to the surface of the leather to preserve its appearance and protect its color. The type of finishing material used is determined by the kind of hide and its eventual use. Top-quality full grain leathers are lightly coated with transparent finishes. "Naked" leathers have no applied finish. For a more opaque finish, pigments are added to the finishing material. Finishes can be very sophisticated and produce a variety of effects, one of which even renders the leather washable.

Pressure and heat are used in the *plating* step. Carried out in conjunction with finishing, plating smooths the surface and increases adhesion of the finishing coat just applied. Rather like ironing, this is the final step to affect the hand and appearance of the finished product. These two processes may be repeated until the desired effects are achieved.

At this point leather might be embossed with specially engraved plates that impress a particular pattern or grain. An example of this is an alligator pattern embossed onto cowhide.

The finish on these lambskins is slightly stiff, with an attractive sheen. They are very suitable for jackets, coats, and the like.

This selection of printed and embossed pigskins illustrates the diverse choices available to the home sewer. Just think of the design potential!

Distressed lambskin works well for a softly tailored suit. The contrast piping also is lambskin, and ostrich is used for accent. A leather-covered D-ring provides the closure on the overlapping layers of the jacket peplum. See pattern information, page 124.

DETAIL: The natural edge of the ostrich skin was used on the peplum.

The final two steps in the tanning process are *grading* and *measuring*. Leather is graded by quality, determined by its hand, thickness, and surface appearance.

Leather is sold according to its surface area. Unlike textiles, which are measured in linear increments, leather is measured in square feet. Measurement is done by photoelectric cells attached to computers. The area is tallied as the skin or hide passes by, with the measured size stamped on the back of the hide. Like leathers are bundled together and shipped for end use.

These steps constitute the tanning process. Not every step is used on every hide, but each hide is subjected to some combination of these steps. The art of tanning lies in combining the hides and skins with a precise process to produce beautiful leather and suede.

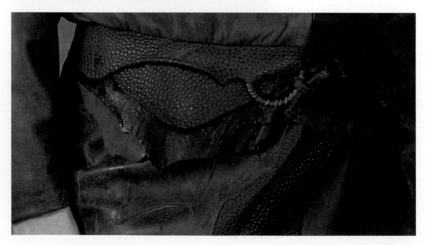

This coarsely grained Australian lamb is fairly heavy, but still soft and pliant. It is the sort of leather often used for bomber style jackets and evokes an image of pilots flying off into the sunset.

CHAPTER 2

Learning About Leather

Leather is the general term for hide or skin with its original fibrous structure more or less intact, tanned or treated to prevent decomposition. The hair or wool may remain on the leather, or it may have been removed. Leather also is made from a hide or skin that has been split into layers before or after tanning.

The term *hide* refers to a whole pelt from a larger animal such as a cow. A *skin* is the pelt from a young animal, or a small animal such as a sheep, calf, goat, or pig. A *kip* is the skin of an animal of the bovine species that is between the sizes of a calf and a mature animal. On pages 124 to 125 you will find pattern information for the finished garments featured in this chapter.

Specialty finishes take many forms. The bronze pigskin has been pearlized; the gray and blue lamb were similarly finished. Specialty finishes are more easily damaged by heat and moisture.

Suede is leather that has been finished by buffing the flesh side (opposite the grain side) to produce a nap. This term refers to the napping process and is unrelated to the type of skin used. Suede is sometimes produced from the split layers that remain after the top grain has been removed. Occasionally, both sides of these split layers are sueded, such as in cowhide splits and chamois (see figures 1 and 2).

In the processing of most hides from large animals, it is customary to cut them into two or more smaller sections for easier handling. The nomenclature of the various parts is shown in figure 3.

The green and red skins are Italian lambsuede. The purple Italian lamb has a nubuck finish, produced by lightly buffing the top grain until it takes on a fine nap that looks smoother than suede.

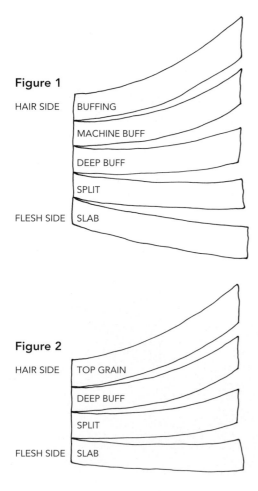

Figure 1

HAIR SIDE — BUFFING

MACHINE BUFF

DEEP BUFF

SPLIT

FLESH SIDE — SLAB

Figure 2

HAIR SIDE — TOP GRAIN

DEEP BUFF

SPLIT

FLESH SIDE — SLAB

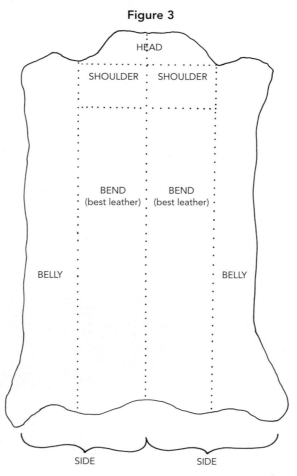

Figure 3

HEAD

SHOULDER   SHOULDER

BEND (best leather)   BEND (best leather)

BELLY   BELLY

SIDE   SIDE

Garment Leathers

Many animals produce suede and leather suitable for garment construction. When the skin of an animal is naturally thick, it often is split to produce lighter weight leather that can be sewn successfully on a home sewing machine. The result is an expanded range of leather from which to choose.

The following describes leather and suede products according to the animal groups from which they are derived. The glossary, page 120, contains additional information about specific kinds of leather and about other animals that produce leather and suede.

Softly folded Italian, Spanish, and New Zealand lambskins show why lamb is such a desirable leather for garments. It is pliant and fine grained. It is available in a variety of weights and finishes that are suitable for garments.

With just a moderate amount of leather you can create an elegant bag that will be a constant companion for years to come. This one is made of cowhide and lined with pigsuede. A zippered pocket at the lining bottom provides secure storage for a passport or other valuables.

PRIMARY CATEGORIES OF LEATHER

CATTLE
steer, cow, calf

LEATHER

garment cow, plongé, calfskin, suede, hair-on calf

CHARACTERISTICS

Cow or calf is relatively inexpensive and has several desirable characteristics. It is strong and durable. It is responsive to any number of specialty finishes that create interesting effects. The larger size of the hide means less piecing of a pattern and less waste. In 2- to 3-ounce weights it is often used for jackets, coats, pants, and handbags. Thinner, supple plongé is a top grain cow with wonderful drape. In is available in weights of 1¾ ounces or less.

PIG and HOG
pig, peccary, carpincho

LEATHERS

Primarily suede

CHARACTERISTICS

Pigsuede is the least expensive of the garment leathers. It is available in many grades, colors, and weights. Garment suede, up to 1½ ounces in weight, is suitable for shirts, pants, skirts, jackets, vests, and handbag linings. These skins are soft with relatively good drape.

DEER FAMILY
deer, elk, antelope, caribou, fallow deer, reindeer

LEATHERS

leather and suede; buckskin

CHARACTERSTICS

In the United States, deerskin and deer suede are more readily available than is leather from other members of this family. "Buckskin" is a general term applied to leather from deer. Only the outer cut from which the surface grain has been removed can accurately be called "genuine buckskin." Buckskin is often used for traditional native American garments. Deerskin and deer suede are available in weights of 2½ ounces or less, and are priced slightly lower than lamb.

SHEEP and LAMB
sheep, lamb, hair skin sheep

LEATHERS

napa leather, suede, chamois, cabretta, shearling, mouton.

CHARACTERISTICS

Lambskin, or napa lamb, is especially soft, with a rich look and feel that give it a distinct character. It is suitable for jackets, coats, pants, skirts, and dresses. Lambsuede has a wonderful draping quality and feels as buttery as silk. It is the premier suede. It works especially well for garments that call for a soft hand, such as blouses, full pants, and flowing skirts. Lamb is more expensive than cow, and is available in weights of 2 ounces or less.

Chamois is sometimes used for garments. It is oil tanned and quite stretchy. Cabretta is a soft, fine-grained, smoothly finished leather often used for gloves as well as garments and handbags.

Shearling and mouton are tanned with the wool intact and may be too heavy for home sewing machines.

GOAT and KID

LEATHERS

Primarily soft leathers

CHARACTERISTICS

Goatskin is soft, but very strong. It is moderately priced and available in a 2-ounce weight. Its beautiful grain and soft feel make it an excellent choice for jackets. Because it tends to stretch, close-fitting garments of goatskin will not keep their shape.

EXOTIC AND FANCY LEATHERS

Aquatic group:
fish, frog, seal, shark, walrus, turtle

Land group:
camel, elephant, ostrich, kangaroo, pangolin

Reptile group:
alligator, crocodile, lizard, snake

CHARACTERISTICS

Many of the leathers in these groups may be too heavy for use with a home sewing machine. The unusual textures and finishes, though, are very appealing. If the weight and hand are light and soft enough, they can be successfully incorporated into spectacular garment designs.

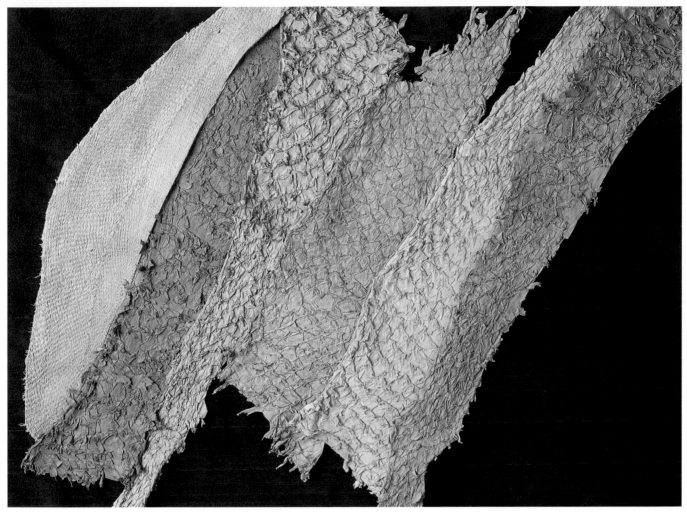

Exotic leather is available in a variety of colors and is most often used for accent or embellishment. The examples are fish skin.

Selecting Leather

Leather and suede are categorized by several factors. Quality is determined by the number and severity of defects in the surface of the hide or skin. The fewer holes, abrasions, and stains, the higher the grade. Grade isn't an indication of how wearable the leather is, but is based upon the skin's visual appeal and the percentage of the skin or hide that can be used. Higher grades have more usable area. Bear in mind that leather is a nat-ural product and some imperfection will always be present. Thin spots are inevitable.

Don't expect the skin or hide to lie entirely flat. Remember that it has been transformed from a three-dimensional to a two-dimensional state.

One of the most important fac-tors in selecting leather or suede for garments is its thickness, expressed in the United States as weight in ounces per square foot. This is an indication of its relative thick-ness. For example, 1 square foot (.093 m) of 1-ounce leather weighs 1 ounce (28 g) and is approximately ¼₆₄ inch (.4 mm) thick; 1 square foot of 3-ounce leather weighs 3 ounces (85 g) and is approximately ¾₆₄ inch (1.2 mm) thick. Leather weights can exceed 10 ounces (28.3 g) per square foot, but such leather is much too heavy for a home sewing machine to penetrate.

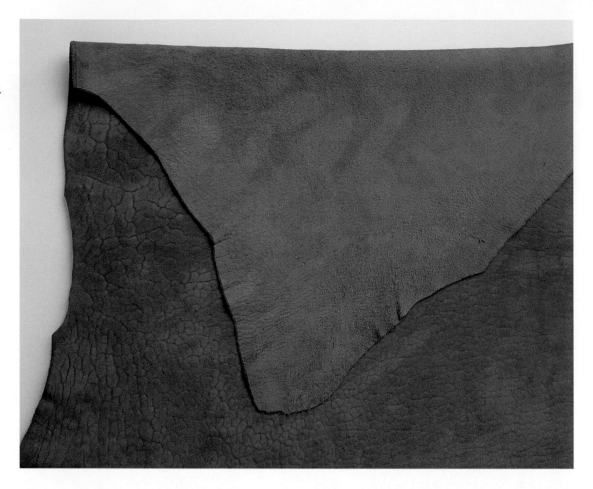

The thickness and soft texture of this Australian nubuck make it a great choice for a jacket.

In Europe, the actual thickness of leather is indicated in millimeters. The chart on page 123 lists leather weights with the corresponding thicknesses.

Home sewing machines can successfully handle leather and suede weighing 2 ounces or less. Some machines will handle leather up to 3 ounces in weight. Leather with a softer, spongier texture—such as lamb—is easier for the needle to penetrate than a stiffer cowhide of the same weight. If you are unsure of your selection, try sewing a seam through three thicknesses of the hide you propose to use. If this seam is satisfactory, your project will probably be successful. If the stitches are uneven or skipped, choose a lighter weight hide or skin, or one with a softer hand. Leather heavier than 1½ ounces is more suitable for outerwear.

Check the leather for defects in the surface, thin areas, or holes. Feel it with your hands. Hold it up to the light to reveal small holes you may not have noticed. Mark these areas with chalk and avoid them or place them in inconspicuous areas of the garment. If you wish to use these areas for other projects, avoid marking on the right side of the leather.

Crocking is the term used to indicate the tendency of color to rub off onto other surfaces. Check for crocking by rubbing a white cloth over sueded surfaces (back and front) of leather. Small particles may rub off the surface of a new skin, but large amounts of color on the cloth indicate a skin to be avoided. *Spewing*, a related problem, occurs when white crystallized or dark gummy deposits from the oily constituents of leather rise to the grain surface. This condition will be visible. Do not use skins or hides that exhibit either condition.

Avoid stiff hides. They may have been tanned or retanned to cover inferior characteristics and will never acquire softness and drape.

If multiple hides are required for a project, purchase them at the same time. Match the dye lot, hand, texture, and appearance.

FABRIC YARDAGE EQUIVALENTS FOR LEATHER

Textiles are sold by the linear yard, and patterns indicate yardage requirements according to the width of the fabric. Leather is sold by the square foot. To accommodate this difference, use the following conversion chart as a guide. Purchase an additional 15 percent to allow for flaws and irregularly shaped skins. For suede, use the yardage required for a napped layout.

For example, if a jacket calls for 3 yards of 45 inch (114 cm) fabric, multiply 3 times 11.25 (1.01) to equal 33.75 square feet (3.03 sq m). Add 15 percent, for a total of 38.75 square feet (3.48 sq m) required for the project.

SIZES OF SKINS AND HIDES

The chart indicates the size range for various hides and skins. It will help you determine the number of skins needed to yield the required yardage for your project.

FABRIC YARDAGE EQUIVALENTS FOR LEATHER

ONE YARD OF FABRIC	APPROXIMATE LEATHER EQUIVALENT
36 inches (91.5 cm) wide	9 square feet (.836 sq m)
45 inches (114 cm) wide	11.25 square feet (1.01 sq m)
54 inches (137 cm) wide	13.5 square feet (1.2 sq m)
60 inches (152.5 cm) wide	15 square feet (1.35 sq m)

SIZES OF SKINS AND HIDES

Garment cow, plongé		
full hide	35–55 square feet	(3.25–5.11 sq m)
sides	18–25 square feet	(1.67–2.32 sq m)
Calf, sheep, cabretta	6–10 square feet	(.56–.93 sq m)
Pig	8–12 square feet	(.74–1.12 sq m)
Goat	6–8 square feet	(.56–.74 sq m)
Kid	3–6 square feet	(.28–.56 sq m)
Lamb	6–8 square feet	(.56–.74 sq m)
Chamois	4–7 square feet	(.37–1.09 sq m)
Deer	7–12 square feet	(1.09–1.12 sq m)
Elk (*full hide*)	55–60 square feet	(5.11–5.57 sq m)
Exotics	*Size varies according to the animal. Exotics are sold differently than other skins. Some are sold by the linear meter, others by different systems of measurement. Not all are suitable for garment use. Some exotics cannot legally be sold in some countries.*	

A shaped hem and self fabric ties add interest to the vest back.

Leather mixes well with a wide variety of fabrics. The color and texture of the pale pigsuede of the vest front combine smoothly with the wools used for the vest back and the skirt. Carefully planned details—matching wool piping and unusual closures—result in a distinctive outfit.

One Hide's Worth, One Skin's Worth

The whole hide from a large animal, such as a cow, can exceed 50 square feet (4.65 sq m). On one occasion we cut an entire suit from a single hide that measured approximately 51.75 square feet (4.81 sq m). The skirt is short, without a waistband, and the long-sleeved jacket ends slightly below the waist The pattern called for 4 yards (3.7 m) of 45 inch (115 cm) fabric.

Since leather has no waste, all the leftover pieces of the hide can be used for other projects. If pants were cut from a hide approximately the same size, enough leather would remain to cut a vest, backpack, or possibly a jacket.

The outer belly and leg areas of the hide are more elastic and less uniform in character. These should not be used for main garment pieces. They will, however, work well as trim and accent pieces such as binding, pockets, collars, cuffs, buttons, and patches.

A pigskin is much smaller than a cowhide, but still delivers a big design punch. Simple unlined vests, such as those illustrated on pages 49 and 52, can be cut from a skin with enough suede left over to make pockets and a collar for a jacket, for example. A purse lining of garment suede is luxurious, and it is inexpensive when made of scraps. Pieced garments can be spectacular.

Small pieces of leather can be used to create a distinctive garment. Here, pigsuede scraps provided the pockets and undercollar on a cotton jacket.

Leather scraps can make wonderful little accents such the tabs on the back of this cotton jacket.

Soft plongé works beautifully for the shawl collar, pockets, and cuffs on a cotton tapestry jacket. On the pockets, raw edges of the hide echo the design lines of the fabric. Lightweight pigsuede insets on the sleeves add color impact.

Traditional jeans gain fashion points when they're made of pigsuede.

CHAPTER 3

Equipment and Supplies

Most of the equipment and supplies used for general sewing can be used to sew suede and leather. Some extra tools are needed, but none are expensive and the use of them will ensure the success of your project and simplify each step of the process.

Sewing Machine and Accessories

A state-of-the-art machine is not required. Any good quality machine can sew garment-weight leather. Consult the manual for recommended settings and accessories. Do try a few sample seams before cutting out an entire project.

Several different presser feet are compatible with leather construction. A Teflon or Teflon-coated foot is the simplest, least costly choice. They are available for almost all machines. A self-adhesive Teflon sheet, available by mail order, can be cut to size and applied to any foot.

An even-feed or walking foot is available for many machines. This foot is handy, but more expensive than a Teflon foot. A specialty leather foot is available for some machines. A roller foot is another option, but it may leave impressions in the leather.

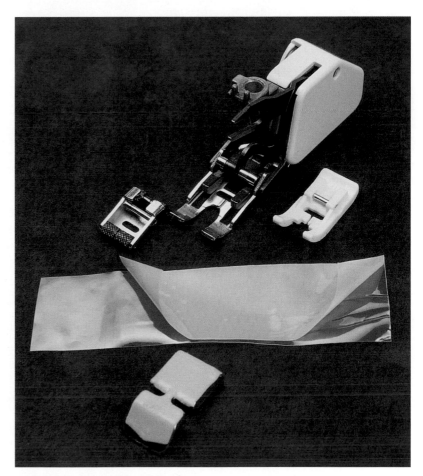

Back row, left to right: a roller foot, walking foot, or Teflon foot all can be used to sew leather and suede. At center is an adhesive-backed Teflon sheet that can be applied to any foot. Teflon has been cut to fit the zipper foot shown in front.

SEWING MACHINE NEEDLES

The correct needles are extremely important in sewing leather. An incorrect or damaged needle will cause skipped stitches and much frustration. Be sure to use the needle type and/or brand that is compatible with your machine—consult the manual if you are unsure. Experiment to find which needle works best for your skins, and begin each project with a new needle.

For very soft lightweight skins, universal needles in size 70/10 or 80/12 are satisfactory. For medium weight or heavier leathers, a special leather needle is required. This needle has a wedge-shaped point that will more easily penetrate the hide. Leather needles are available in several sizes. Size 90/14 is a good choice for medium-weight leathers; heavier leather may require size 100/16 or 110/18.

A needle with a longer, deeper scarf (that dent in the back of the needle eye) can prevent skipped stitches. Some machine manufacturers recommend that leather be sewn with a 90/14 stretch needle or jeans needles in sizes 80/12, 90/14, or 100/16. If skipped stitches remain a problem, try using a strip of tear-away stabilizer under the seam.

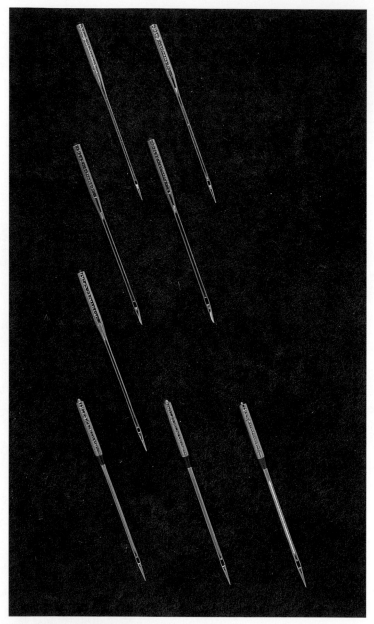

Using the correct needle will eliminate skipped stitches and aggravation.

BACK ROW, left to right: universal point, sizes 70/10 and 80/12.

SECOND ROW: leather needles, sizes 90/14 and 100/16.

THIRD ROW: stretch needle, size 90/14.

FRONT ROW: jeans needles, sizes 90/14, 100/16, and 110/18.

Thread

The best thread to use is good quality, long-staple polyester. There are several brands available, and it comes in a large array of colors and is widely available. Cotton-wrapped polyester thread is another good choice. Do not use 100 percent cotton thread; one of the tanning chemicals used to process the leather will cause it to rot.

Remember that winding polyester thread too quickly onto a bobbin can stretch it. The result is puckered seams as the thread relaxes during stitching.

Bonded nylon is often used commercially for heavier leather, but it is designed for use in industrial machines. It will damage the thread guides of a home machine and is too large in diameter to flow smoothly through even a large needle. Nylon also develops static electricity.

For topstitching, use polyester topstitching thread or two strands of regular polyester sewing thread. To avoid tangles when topstitching with two strand of thread, wind both onto bobbins. This way all thread feeds through the machine in the same direction.

Polyester and cotton-wrapped polyester threads are best for machine stitching on leather. Glovers' needles (above) simplify hand stitching. The triangular wedge-shaped tip more easily penetrates leather. For beading, number 12 sharps are a good choice.

Cutting Tools

The preferred method for cutting leather is a sharp rotary cutter and cutting mat. Keep the rotary blades in top condition with a sharpener made for this purpose. Sharp scissors can also be used for cutting.

Avoid using pins in leather. Skins are difficult to penetrate, and pins will leave permanent holes. Instead, use weights to secure the pattern for cutting. If the weights have spikes on them, flip them over to avoid punctures.

Small trimming scissors such as appliqué scissors or tailors' points scissors are used for trimming and snipping during garment construction. Like other cutting tools, these must be kept sharp.

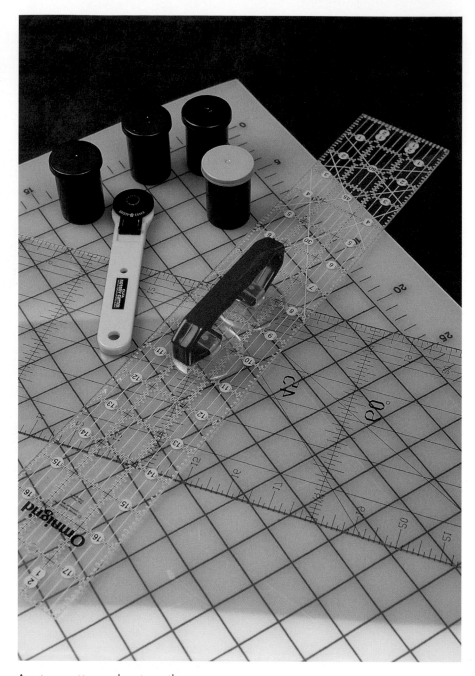

A rotary cutter and mat are the most efficient means of cutting leather and suede. Film canisters filled with sand make good pattern weights.

Pressing Equipment

An iron is used less in the construction of leather garments than for those made of fabric. Use a press cloth of plain brown kraft paper. In most cases a dry iron works best, set at a medium temperature. Some leathers, particularly lambsuede and pigsuede, may tolerate steam. Always do test samples. The finishes on embossed and specialty finished leathers are produced with heat and pressure and can be damaged by ironing.

Much of the "pressing" done during construction is accomplished with a *rubber*, *rawhide*, or *wooden mallet*. An alternative is to wrap a hammer with a piece of the garment leather. Exercise caution with this method as too much force can leave impressions on the garment.

A *seam stick*—a half-round length of smoothly sanded hardwood—provides a firm base upon which to press seams open with a mallet. Just as in tailoring fabric, this method eliminates impressions of the seam allowance on the right side of the garment. A small wooden *wallpaper seam roller* is handy for flattening glued areas.

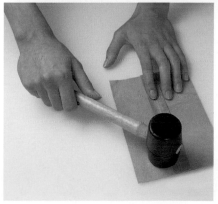

A seam stick makes it possible to press seams perfectly. A mallet, rather than an iron, is most often used for pressing.

A marble slab, shown on page 31, provides a smooth, stable, and solid base for pounding with a mallet. Any surface with these qualities can be used, but if you intend to do a lot of leather work, the marble is a good investment. An optimum size is 12 inches (30 cm) square and 1 inch (2.5 cm) thick.

Hand Sewing Tools

The triangular-tipped *glover's needle* is best for hand sewing. The size range for garment use is approximately 5 through 7. As for sewing with fabric, choose the smallest size that will accomplish the task. Wax and press the thread for smooth stitching.

For beading, use a *nickel-plated steel needle*, size 12 sharp. Because leather is tougher to penetrate than fabric, a long, thin beading needle won't do the job. The size 12 needle can accommodate nylon thread in size 00 or A. The primary consideration in beading is the size of the hole in the bead, so it may be necessary to make an adjustment in the needle size.

Apply *beeswax* to hand sewing thread for smoother stitching, then iron it between paper towels or an old cloth to embed the wax in the thread fibers. There will be fewer tangles and knots when you sew.

An *awl* is useful for piercing holes to facilitate hand sewing. Use one with a very sharp point.

Tools and supplies that are particularly useful for working with leather include (clockwise from bottom) a ballpoint pen and permanent marking pens, Hera marker, awl, button shank spacer, appliqué scissors, punch, dental floss (for sewing buttons), chalk wheels, fusible and sew-in seam tapes.

Useful Notions and Supplies

Pins are not used with leather as they don't easily penetrate the skin and they do leave permanent holes. Instead, use small *binder clips* to hold garment pieces together during construction. The small ones are inexpensive, easy to manage, won't shift, and can be placed within the seam allowance so that no permanent impressions are left on the garment right side. An alternative is to staple pieces together ¼ inch (.5 cm) from the cut edges. Clothespins or paper clips also can be used.

A Japanese *Hera*, a marking tool originally made of bone and now usually plastic, is used to make impressions on leather. Its advantage is that it leaves no residue that might stain leather or suede.

The *chalk wheel*—a chalk dispenser with a rotating wheel—makes fine, precise lines. Always test to be sure the chalk will brush off before using it on the right side of the leather or suede.

A standard *ballpoint pen* can be used to mark pattern construction details, such as darts, on the wrong side of the leather.

Permanent markers with fine tips also can be used to mark construction details. A broader-tipped marker in a matching color is handy for touching up flaws in the leather and coloring edges.

Glue stick is used instead of stitched basting to form temporary bonds during construction. It is not used where permanent bonds are desired.

Double-sided tape sometimes is used to secure garment pieces during construction. Select a variety that can be sewn. Adhesives on some of these tapes can cause stitching difficulty; these should be used only in the seam allowances.

Hems and other finishing steps are done with *permanent contact cement.* This is a neoprene-based glue such as rubber cement. For most satisfactory results, use a nonstringing formula. Thin the cement with a solvent that contains toluene. Follow package directions for use of both the cement and thinner. Be aware that chemicals used in dry cleaning can weaken the bond.

Working with leather calls for a few additional sewing room supplies. Glue stick, basting tape, and binder clips replace pins to hold pieces for stitching. A wooden wallpaper seam roller and rubber, rawhide, or wooden mallet help smooth seams; the marble slab under them provides a firm surface upon which to work. Permanent contact cements fix seam allowances and hems in place.

CHAPTER 4

Special Techniques for Leather and Suede

Sewing with leather and suede is not the least bit difficult, but does require some adaptations of technique. Take time to sew a few samples before you begin a project.

PRESSER FEET AND FEED MECHANISMS

A Teflon-coated presser foot is the best choice for sewing leather and suede. It is a must for topstitching, and can also handle regular construction stitching and decorative stitching. It is less expensive and less cumbersome than other feet that might be used. Not having to change the foot repeatedly saves time and aggravation. Several other presser foot options are discussed on page 25.

Leather and suede are spongy. Because of this characteristic, leather will pass across the feed dogs more evenly if there is less pressure on the presser foot. On some machines manual adjustment is possible. Other machines automatically make this adjustment internally. A few older machines have preset pressure settings and cannot be adjusted.

BEFORE YOU SEW

Basting is best done with a glue stick. It is temporary, easy, and fast. Use a brand that you like for sewing fabrics. Apply the glue only in the seam allowances; it does not dry clear and will remain visible.

Binder clips also are used for some basting as well as for general construction. Pins do not easily penetrate most leather or suede and will leave permanent holes.

NEEDLE CHOICE

Needles are very important in successful construction. It is usually best to use a needle designed especially for sewing leather; it will penetrate skins and hides more easily. Skipped stitches are often the result of incorrect needle selection, and changing to a larger needle size may solve the problem. If there are still skipped stitches, try using a strip of tear-away stabilizer under the leather or between the presser foot and the leather. For a seam that has just a few skipped stitches, fill in the missing ones by hand, using the existing holes as a guide. For more information about needles, see page 26.

STITCH LENGTH

Needle holes in leather and suede are permanent. Do test samples of stitch length before beginning the project. Stitches placed too close together can work like perforations in a tablet of paper; the seam allowance will tear off and the garment will disassemble. The customary range of stitch lengths for sewing leather on a home machine is 7 to 12 per inch. Softer, lighter weight leathers and suedes are stitched at 10 to 12 stitches per inch. Mid-weight leathers, those in the 1½ to 2 ounce range, are stitched at 8 to 10 stitches per inch. Heavier leathers are stitched with 8 or fewer stitches per inch. Again, always stitch samples to determine what length is best for each project.

Stitching Tips

Use directional stitching for less distortion. Stitch from the widest to the narrowest point, and from the bottom to the top (figure 4.1).

Whizzing along may be normal for most sewing, but if speed is reduced while sewing on leather there is less chance for error. The needle has more time to properly form a stitch. Slower stitching gives more control of the material going through the stitching mechanism so that it is less likely to stray from the intended stitching line.

To secure the beginning and end of a stitching line, tie the thread ends in a square knot or dressmaker's knot (figure 4.2). A very small dot of seam sealant on the knot will assure its longevity. Leave a tail on the tied thread ends and cement or stitch them into the seam finish. Backstitching is not advisable unless stitches can be made using exactly the same holes as the forward stitches. If extra holes are created, weak or perforated seams will result.

Feed dogs can mar leather surfaces. To prevent marks, use paper or tear-away stabilizer between the feed dogs and the leather. Marks sometimes can be disguised—see Finishing Tips, page 35.

Holes in leather are permanent. Seams cannot be let out. They can be taken in, but if subsequent stitching lines are too close to the original stitching, the seam may tear out. To prevent torn seams in underarm and crotch curves, stretch the seams slightly as you sew to build in a bit of wearing ease.

When finishing curved seams like pockets, collars, crotch or armscye, make small clips or clip away small notches in the seam allowance before turning and cementing. Exercise restraint. Additional notches can be cut if necessary, but they can't be replaced (figures 4.3 and 4.4).

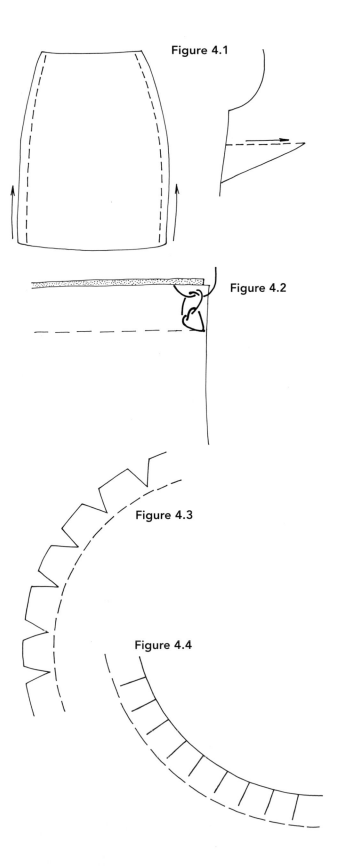

Figure 4.1

Figure 4.2

Figure 4.3

Figure 4.4

On curves or other points of stress (the leather's, not yours!) apply preshrunk linen or rayon tape along the seamline. Baste it over the seamline with glue stick, one edge ⅛ inch (3 mm) over the stitching line and the remainder extending into the seam allowance. Stitch, clipping as necessary to release tension. Fusible seam tape in narrow widths is handy to use. Secure it with the tip of the iron, then stitch.

Sharp corners, such as collar points, do not turn neatly. Round them if possible for better results. An alternative method for stitching points on collars is described on page 72.

When joining leather to fabric, sew with the leather on the bottom. The feed dogs tend to pull it along for a smoother application.

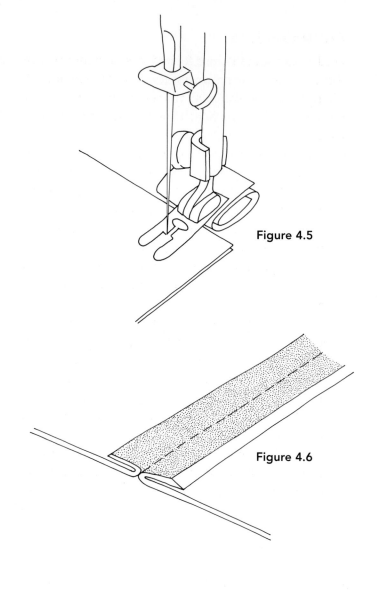

Figure 4.5

DEALING WITH LEATHER'S THICKNESS

When crossing thick seams, fold a piece of fabric or use a special tool behind and under the presser foot to keep it level as you stitch. This will help prevent skipped stitches (figure 4.5).

Reducing bulk is the name of the game. Each seam allowance is *skived* (pronounced SKYV'd), or graded, to create a beveled edge. Hold the scissors at about a 45-degree angle and trim (figure 4.6).

Figure 4.6

Occasionally it will be difficult to reach a spot with your machine, or the layers may be too thick for the needle to penetrate. When this happens, use a glover's needle and waxed thread to do a hand backstitch (figure 4.7). Waxing the thread will prevent tangles and snarls. Press the waxed thread between pieces of fabric to embed wax into the thread fibers.

Figure 4.7

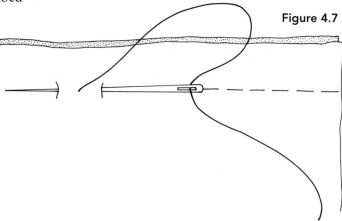

Pressing

Leather and suede do not tolerate heat and moisture in the same way that textiles do. The combination of heat, pressure, and moisture must be modified when pressing leather. Working with fusible interfacing is discussed on page 64.

Use a dry iron set at a moderate temperature. Do not use a Teflon ironing board cover; it reflects heat back into the leather. Plain brown kraft paper makes a good press "cloth." Grocery bags can be used for this purpose, but avoid printed areas; the ink can transfer to the leather. Leather can be pressed on either side.

Leather that has been stored folded rather than rolled may have marks or creases that cannot be removed. Most wrinkles will hang out.

To press constructions details such as seams and darts, finger press and tap with a mallet over a flat or curved surface, whichever is appropriate. This pressing is made permanent by either stitching or permanently cementing the seam allowance or detail into position. With bulky leather, first deaden the seam allowances by pounding with a mallet.

Further information about pressing specific kinds of seams and construction details can be found at those headings. Pressing equipment is described on page 29.

Finishing Tips

On suede, marks such as those made by the feed dog teeth can be made less noticeable by rubbing with a scrap of the suede, sueded sides together. This technique can also conceal needle holes. On smooth leather, cover marks by rubbing with a bit of shoe polish in the same color.

To make cut edges less noticeable, color with permanent marking pen that matches the leather color. This trick works well for buttonhole slits and lapped seams where a raw edge is exposed.

To Sum Up

For successful sewing on leather and suede, remember a few basic rules. These are the guidelines that will always be followed in some form or another.

1.
Use an appropriate presser foot.

2.
If possible, reduce the presser-foot pressure.

3.
Use a needle that is appropriate for the weight of the leather.

4.
Lengthen the stitch.

5.
Reduce sewing speed.

Seams for Leather and Suede

The following section describes specific seams, and the methods used to produce them. Of course, not every seam is used in every garment. Use the one(s) best suited to your particular project, and be consistent. Interesting seam finishes can be part of the overall design or a specially featured element.

Consider the function of the garment and select seams strong enough to withstand the wear it will receive. Contrasting thread brings the seam forward visually. Does the garment have a sporty feel? Garments of this type often incorporate topstitching into the design. Do the seams require extra strength? Consider using mock welt seams, which have two to three stitching lines and can withstand a great deal of stress. Make several sample seams with the leather, then decide which is the most desirable. Use the tools and equipment as described in Chapter 3.

PLAIN SEAM

This is the most basic seam for construction. It is the seam of choice for dressmaker applications when lightweight suede or leather is used. When a soft look is desired, as in a lambsuede blouse for example, do not cement the seam allowances.

If necessary, apply seam tape as described under Stitching Tips, page 33. With right sides together, stitch along the seamline leaving thread tails at the beginning and end of the seam. Tie ends in a square or dressmaker's knot (figure 4.2, page 33). For medium to heavy leather, pound the seam allowances to reduce bulk. Clip or notch seam allowances as necessary. Place the seam over a seam stick and finger press it open (photo 1).

Pound along the seamline with a mallet, lightly for lightweight leather and suede, more firmly for medium and heavier leather (photo 2).

Skive the seam allowance edges to reduce bulk (photo 3).

Photo 1

Photo 2

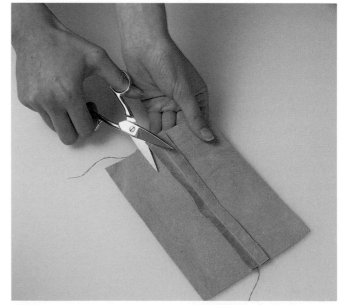
Photo 3

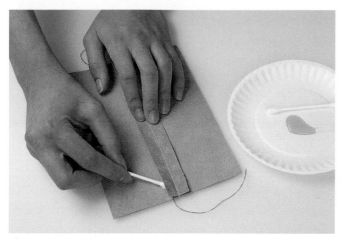

Photo 4

With a brush, syringe, or applicator such as a cotton swab, apply permanent contact cement to the underside of each seam allowance. Apply a thin, even coat and do not extend the cement to the edge of the seam allowance. This way, the glue will not leak beyond the seam allowance or soak through to the surface (photo 4). Tuck thread ends under the seam allowance.

Finger press the seam allowances in place, lift seam allowances to release tension, then finger press again (photo 5).

For heavier leathers, pound lightly with a mallet on a flat surface (photo 6). Let the piece dry.

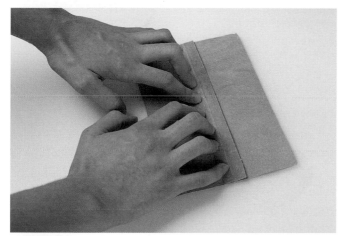

Photo 5

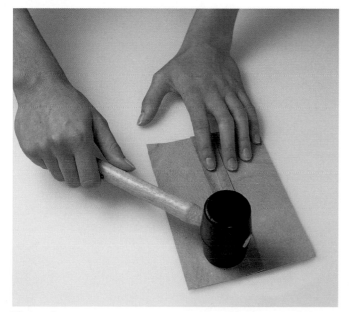

Photo 6

Photo 7

TOPSTITCHED PLAIN SEAM

This sportswear finish is used on light- to medium-weight leather to strengthen the seam and control the seam allowances. Construct as for a plain seam, but instead of pressing the seam open, finger press both seam allowances to one side. Tap with a mallet. On heavier leather, deaden the seam allowances by pounding with a mallet. Then proceed as for the plain seam. Tuck thread ends into the seam and secure with a dab of glue.

On the right side, stitch $\frac{1}{16}$ inch (2 mm) from the seamline through the surface layer and both seam allowances. The inner edge of the presser foot is a good stitching guide. Trim and grade as previously described. Topstitching holds the seam allowances in place without cementing (photo 7).

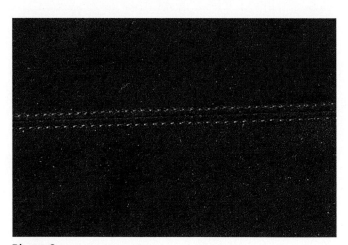

Photo 8

PLAIN SEAM WITH DOUBLE TOPSTITCHING

An alternative sportswear finish, this one often is seen in handbags or skirts. The seam looks tidy, and its bulk is reduced. Construct as for the plain seam, pressing the seam open with fingers or mallet over a seam stick. Skive the seam allowances. On the right side, stitch $\frac{1}{16}$ inch (2 mm) to each side of the seamline, tucking the thread ends into the seam (photo 8).

FLAT-FELLED SEAM

This seam is self-enclosed, leaving no unfinished edges. It is very strong, making it a good choice for sportswear. Try this shortcut technique to simplify the process.

Fold and pound one seam allowance to the wrong side along the seamline. With wrong sides together, slide the piece to be joined snugly into the fold (photo 9). Use glue stick under the seam allowance to hold in position. The raw edge of the second piece should be touching the inner fold.

Sew 1/16 inch (2 mm) from the raw edge of the folded seam allowance (figure 4.8, photo 10). Tie the thread ends.

Pull the lower layer open to the left. Fold and pound the seam allowance area to the right. Glue baste into position (figure 4.9).

Topstitch 1/16 inch (2 mm) from the fold (photo 11).

Be sure to stitch like seams so they lie in the same direction; for example, both shoulder seams should face forward.

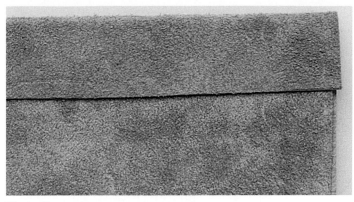

Photo 9

Photo 10

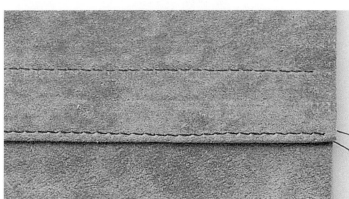

Photo 11

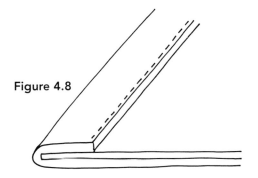

Figure 4.8

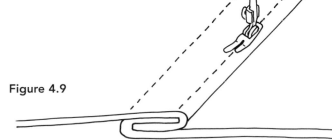

Figure 4.9

MOCK WELT SEAM

Construct as for a plain seam. Press both seam allowances to one side with a mallet. Topstitch ⅛ inch (3 mm) from the seamline. A second row of topstitching may be added, if desired, ¼ inch (.5 cm) from the first row. Trim and grade the seam allowances (photos 12 and 13).

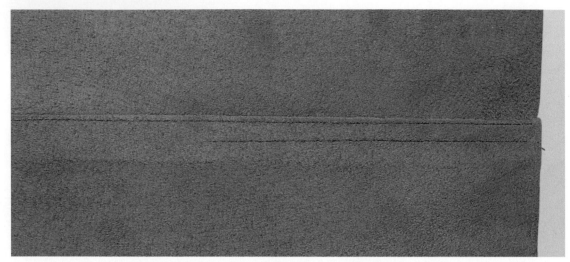

Photo 12
Mock welt seam, wrong side

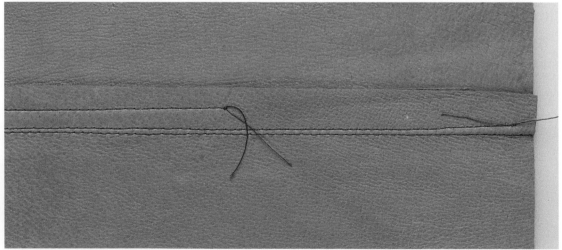

Photo 13
Mock welt seam, right side

LAPPED SEAM, METHOD 1

A variety of lapped seams are used in design and construction, particularly with medium to heavy leathers such as cowhide.

Mark the seamline on one piece with a Hera marker or chalk wheel. On the corresponding piece, turn under along the seamline, secure with glue stick, and pound with a mallet. Lap the folded edge over the marked edge, aligning the fold with the marked seamline. Glue baste in place. Topstitch ¹⁄₁₆ inch (2 mm) from the folded edge. A second row of topstitching may be added ¼ inch (7 mm) from the first row. Trim and grade the seam allowances (photos 14 and 15).

Photo 14
Method 1 lapped seam, wrong side

Photo 15
Method 1 lapped seam, right side

LAPPED SEAM, METHOD 2

This method works especially well with heavy leather. Omit the seam allowance on the overlapping piece. Cut the standard seam allowance on the underlying piece, and mark the seamline with a Hera marker or chalk wheel.

Place the overlapping seamline edge exactly along the marked seamline on the corresponding piece. Glue baste and topstitch ⅛ inch (3 mm) from the seamline edge. A second row of topstitching can be added ¼ inch (.5 cm) from the first row. Trim excess seam allowance from the underlying piece (photos 15 and 16).

Photo 15
Method 2 lapped seam, wrong side

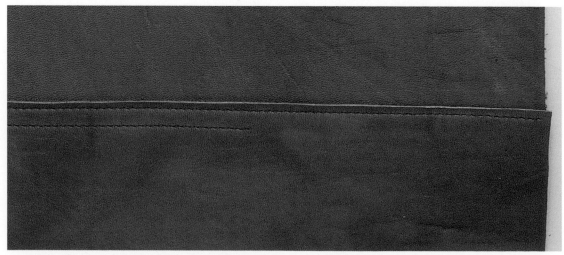

Photo 16
Method 2 lapped seam, right side

SLOT SEAM, METHOD 1

Slot seams can function as a design element in general construction and can be used to join bulky pieces attractively. A coordinating or contrasting strip of leather or textile is placed under the seam and the two garment sections are sewn to the strip. Care must be taken to keep the seam-line orientation of the two pieces the same as it would have been had a conventional seam been used.

On each garment piece, fold under the seam allowance plus half the intended visible width of the insert. Pound, and glue baste. Glue baste in position in the desired position on the strip, then stitch close to the fold. Trim and grade the seam allowances to reduce bulk (photo 17).

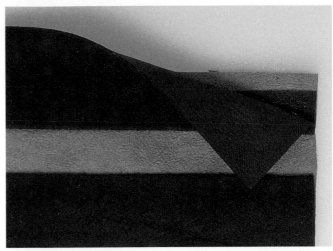

Photo 17
Method 1 slot seam

SLOT SEAM, METHOD 2

This is essentially the same as Method 1, except that the seam allowance and half the width to be exposed is trimmed away rather than being folded under. Glue baste in position on the strip, then stitch (photos 18 and 19).

Photo 18
Method 2 slot seam, wrong side

Photo 19
Method 2 slot seam, right side

CHAPTER 5

Projects to Get You Started

A simple wardrobe accessory or quick garment can get you hooked on sewing with leather and give you confidence to tackle a more complicated design. Before you begin, familiarize yourself with the basic stitches and techniques described in Chapter 4 by stitching up some samples from scraps of the leather you intend to use. Take liberties with these designs, too! Try some of the embellishments described in Chapter 8 to create a distinctive design of your own. You will find pattern information for these projects on pages 124 to 125.

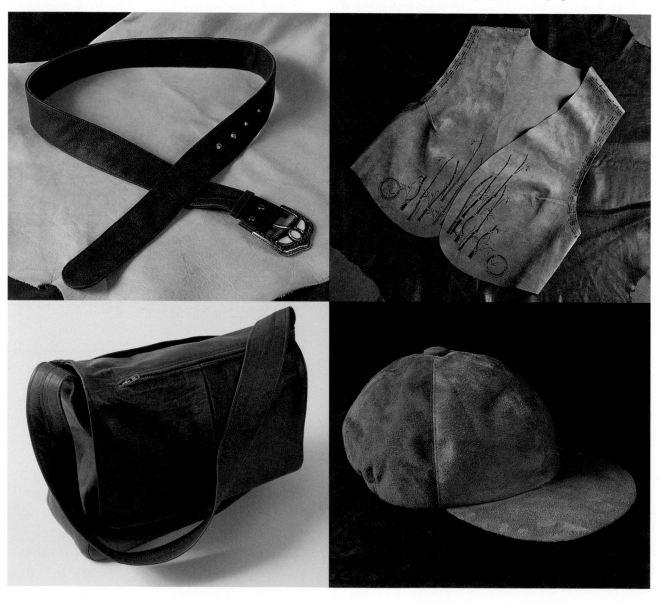

Belts

A belt adds instant panache to the simplest ensemble. It provides a visual transition between top and bottom, creating an impression that can vary from elegant refinement to exuberant frivolity. A belt can be made in a short period of time and takes little in the way of material, but a new one can create a big impact.

Anyone can wear a belt. Remember that under a jacket the eye sees just the suggestion of a waistline, not the actual dimension. For the most satisfactory results, keep the design in scale with your size and shape.

Remember, too, that a woman's garments button right over left, so the belt buckle is usually on the left and the overlapping or looping portion is on the right. The opposite is true for men.

Soft Suede Tie

A simply styled, versatile belt is a great addition to any wardrobe. The rough texture of suede helps hold a knot in place and keep the ends tucked in place.

The material you choose will determine whether your own version is elegant, such as the one shown, or fashionably funky. You might like to vary the width and shape of the ends, or to piece together different colors of suede for design punch. Lace the edges with thin strips of suede for a different effect. As another variation, make the belt lining from suede in a contrasting color.

Soft pigsuede makes an attractive belt that's comfortable to wear over an elastic-waist skirt. We've tied this one in back for a smoother look.

SUPPLIES

• Pigsuede, 1 to 1½ ounce weight, 4 square feet (.37 sq m)

• Matching polyester or cotton-wrapped polyester thread

CUTTING

Note: It may be necessary to piece the leather to the desired size.

1. Cut a piece of suede 3 to 4 inches (7.5 to 10 cm) wide plus two seam allowances, and, in length, the waist measurement plus 14 to 18 inches (36 to 46 cm), plus seam allowances. Shape the ends as desired.

2. Cut the lining the same size from the same or a lighter weight suede.

CONSTRUCTION

1. With right sides together, stitch the belt to the lining, leaving an opening at the center for turning. Knot the threads to secure the seams.

2. Trim and grade the seam allowances. Turn right side out. Pound the edges.

3. Cement the opening with permanent contact cement.

4. Topstitch if desired.

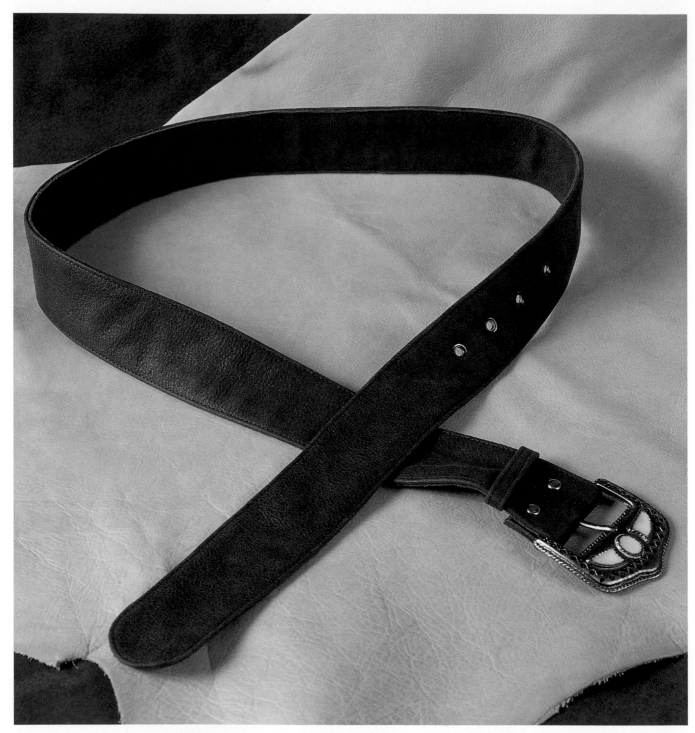

Timeless styling and quality materials make
a belt that will be treasured for a lifetime.

Traditional Belt

A classic belt, in this case featuring an attractive metal buckle, is a mainstay in almost any wardrobe. Traditionally, the buckle is sewn or riveted to one end of the belt. The holes for the prong, at the other end, are reinforced with metal eyelets. A small loop acts as a keeper for the loose end. This system works well with heavier leather, or when the belt is heavily interfaced.

Cap rivets are the metal studs used to secure the buckle to the belt (figure 5.1). They are available in a variety of finishes, and in lengths to accommodate different thicknesses of belting material. Install them according to the manufacturer's instructions.

SUPPLIES

- Leather, 2-ounce weight, enough to make two strips the length of the waist measurement plus approximately 7 inches (18 cm) plus two seam allowances. Use different leather for the lining, if desired.
- Matching polyester or cotton-wrapped polyester thread
- Buckle
- Cap rivets, applicator tool, hammer, and punch pliers
- Glue stick
- Metal eyelets, gripper pliers
- Stiff interfacing, if desired, cut to the size of the belt

CUTTING

1. Determine the finished length and width of the belt. The length should include approximately 2 inches (5 cm) for the buckle attachment and 5 inches (12.5 cm) beyond the waist measurement for adjustment and design balance. Add seam allowances.

2. Cut one belt and one lining section.

3. Cut interfacing, if used, to the finished size of the belt, eliminating the seam allowances.

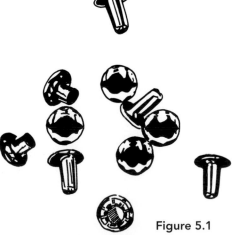

Figure 5.1

CONSTRUCTION

1. Glue baste the interfacing to the wrong side of the outer belt section.

2. Fold under and pound the seam allowances. Glue baste in place.

3. Place the belt over the lining, wrong sides together. Glue baste. Topstitch around the edges. Trim away the lining seam allowances close to the stitching.

4. Cut a small slit or hole 2 inches (5 cm) from the buckle end. Install the buckle. Sew the end in place or attach it with cap rivets.

5. Mark positions for metal eyelets at the waist measurement and at 1 inch (2.5 cm) intervals on either side. Use punch pliers to make the smallest possible hole that the eyelet will penetrate. Use gripper pliers to install the eyelets.

6. Make and install a small keeper loop to support the loose end of the belt.

Belt Variation

For a variation on the theme, vary the width of the belt and replace the buckle with a leather-wrapped D-ring. The concha belt shown here was slipped onto a thin leather strip. Then the strip was riveted to the larger piece, with the rivets hidden under the conchas.

Soft pigsuede makes a comfortable vest. Bust darts prevent gaping at the front of the armscye. The stenciled design is easy to apply and adds a beautiful accent. For tips on stenciling, see page 113.

Unlined Vests

One of the simplest beginning leather projects is an unlined pigsuede vest. Most sizes can be made from a single skin with scraps left over for other projects. Since pigsuede doesn't ravel, edge finishes are unnecessary. Stenciling, stitching, applique, reverse applique, buttons, or piecing can produce spectacular effects. Additional possibilities are illustrated in this chapter. A vest is a quick and welcome gift.

Choose a simple pattern and make the necessary pattern adjustments to assure a proper fit. A comfortable fit in textile will also be comfortable in the leather. But darts will eliminate gaping at the armscye in front. Shoulder darts will eliminate gaping at the armscye in back. Check with a good book on pattern fitting. The key to success is a well-fitted pattern.

This vest is unlined for simplicity. If you wish to line the vest, read about the options on page 95.

Stenciled Vest

SUPPLIES

- Simple vest pattern, adjusted to fit
- Pigskin, 1½ ounce weight, 12 square feet (1.12 sq m)
- Polyester or cotton-wrapped polyester thread to match
- Embellishment supplies, as desired

CUTTING

Use a layout as for napped fabric. Eliminate seam allowance except at the shoulders and sides.

CONSTRUCTION

1. Embellish the flat pieces as desired.

2. Stitch the darts. Leave long thread tails, and knot them securely with a square knot or tailor's knot. Pound to press and cement, tucking thread tails under the darts.

3. With right sides together, stitch the shoulder and side seams. Knot the thread ends as you did for the darts.

4. Trim the seam allowances at an angle, and finger press them open. Pound and permanently cement the seam allowances and darts, tucking the thread ends underneath.

A reversible vest features a stenciled design on one side and charms sewn to the other. After embellishment, the two lightweight suede layers were joined using a decorative machine stitch.

Lightweight pigsuede was pieced, then stenciled, for a vest that's compatible with several outfits.

For quick embellishment, the buttons are glued in place, not sewn. Lengths of silk ribbon are threaded through additional buttons and sewn into the shoulder seams. Always test the glue on a scrap before using it on the garment itself.

ABOVE: Reverse appliqué and bead fringe are featured on this modification of the basic vest project on page 50.

LEFT: The simplest vest serves as a backdrop for all sorts of artistic experimentation and leather combinations. This unlined vest is pieced with traditionally finished pigsuede and one with a specialty finish, then decorated with stenciled geckos. The bead eyes are glued in place.

Purses

High-quality purses are expensive and almost never seem to have the features that make them just right. To get the perfect bag, modify one that fits and functions well.

The beloved bag shown here had reached the end of its useful life, and was made by a company no longer in business. The shape and size are terrific. We used the old bag as the model for a new one, but added a soft deer-suede lining. The finished bag is 12½ inches (32 cm) wide, 11 inches (28 cm) high, and 5 inches (13 cm) deep at the bottom.

A well-used bag offered several favorite features that were incorporated into the new version. A roomy flap pocket zips closed for security, and the wide shoulder strap provides wearing comfort.

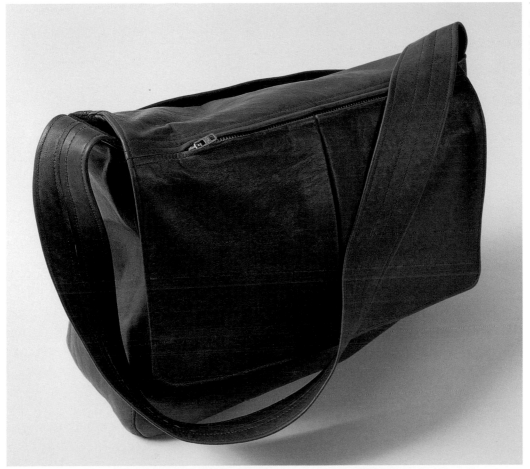

The bag was remade in soft, 2-ounce glazed lamb, the color similar to that of the original model.

Purse with Zipper

SUPPLIES

- Leather, 2 ounce weight, 10 square feet (.93 sq m)
- Deersuede or pigsuede, 1 ounce weight, 8 square feet (.74 sq m)
- Polyester or cotton-wrapped polyester thread to match
- Heavy-duty brass or nylon zipper, 9 inches (22.5 cm)

CUTTING

Cut pieces according to the diagrams, figures 5.2 through 5.10. Seam and hem allowances are included. Use a template to round the corners, making them identical throughout. Check the strap length before cutting and adjust if necessary.

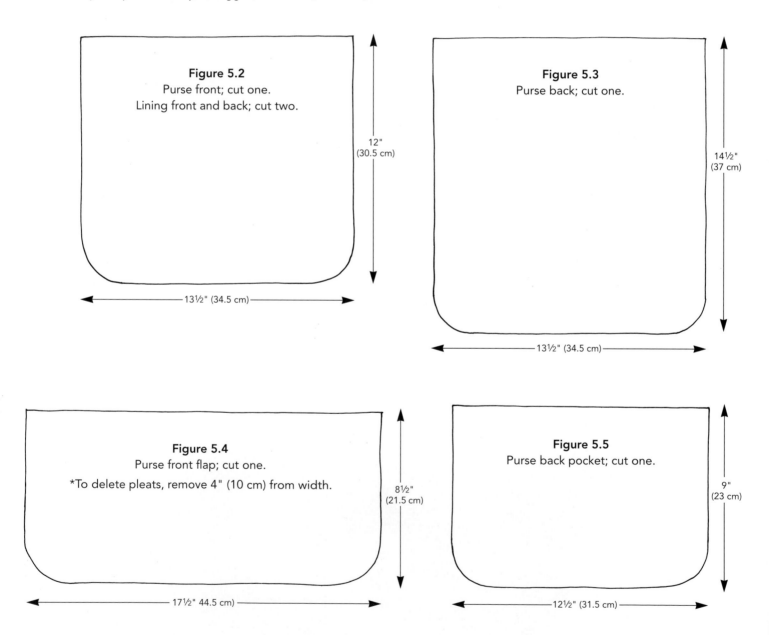

Figure 5.2
Purse front; cut one.
Lining front and back; cut two.

12" (30.5 cm)

13½" (34.5 cm)

Figure 5.3
Purse back; cut one.

14½" (37 cm)

13½" (34.5 cm)

Figure 5.4
Purse front flap; cut one.
*To delete pleats, remove 4" (10 cm) from width.

8½" (21.5 cm)

17½" 44.5 cm)

Figure 5.5
Purse back pocket; cut one.

9" (23 cm)

12½" (31.5 cm)

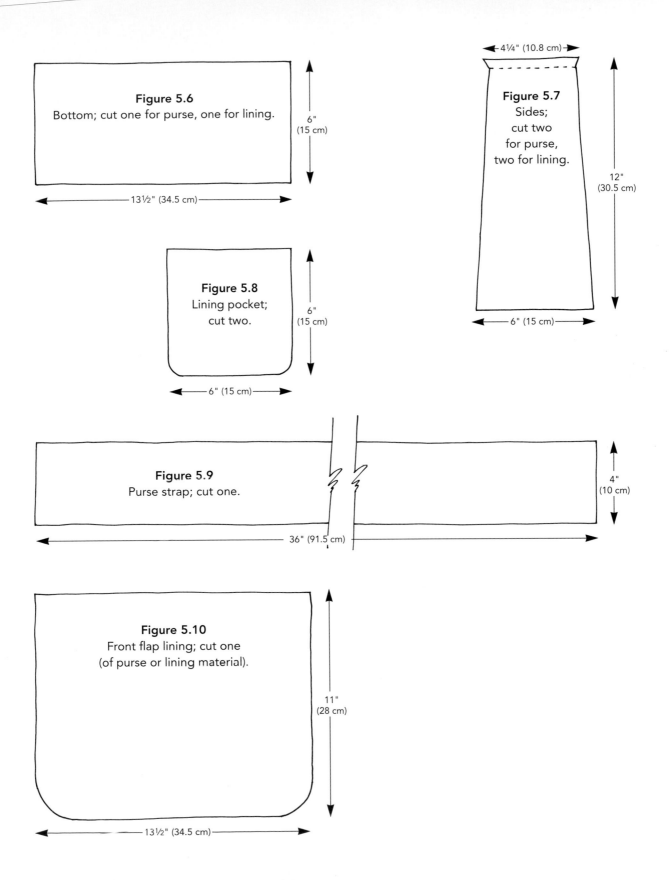

Figure 5.6
Bottom; cut one for purse, one for lining.

6"
(15 cm)

13½" (34.5 cm)

Figure 5.7
Sides;
cut two
for purse,
two for lining.

4¼" (10.8 cm)

12"
(30.5 cm)

6" (15 cm)

Figure 5.8
Lining pocket;
cut two.

6"
(15 cm)

6" (15 cm)

Figure 5.9
Purse strap; cut one.

4"
(10 cm)

36" (91.5 cm)

Figure 5.10
Front flap lining; cut one
(of purse or lining material).

11"
(28 cm)

13½" (34.5 cm)

CONSTRUCTION

Seam allowances are ½ inch (1.3 cm) except as noted. At seam ends, knot the thread ends.

Back Pocket

1. Fold under and pound the seam allowance on the curved sides. Notch the curves as necessary. Glue baste.

2. Fold down the upper edge 1 inch (2.5 cm); pound. Permanently cement in place.

3. Position the pocket on the right side of the purse back. Glue baste just under the side and lower edges to hold in place. Stitch close to the pocket edge around the curved sides, stitching a triangle at each upper corner for reinforcement.

Flap Pocket Zipper

1. On the purse back, fold down the top seam allowance and pound.

2. Fold and pound 1 inch (2.5 cm) pleats in the purse flap. Fold down and pound the seam allowance on the top edge (figure 5.11).

3. Place the purse back and flap with right sides together. Mark the center 9 inches (23 cm). Sew from each mark to the outer edge (figure 5.12).

4. Finger press the seam open. Glue baste the seam allowances to hold them in place (figure 5.13).

5. Center the zipper under the opening, right side facing outward. Glue baste. Topstitch each side ¼ inch (7 mm) from the fold (figure 5.14).

Sides and Bottom

1. With right sides together, sew the wide end of each side piece to the bottom. Finger press the seams open. Pound and glue baste them.

2. With right sides together, clip the side/bottom piece to the back/flap section. Stitch along the seamline, stopping ½ inch (1.3 cm) from the upper edges of the sides. Stitch again ⅛ inch (3 mm) from the seamline through the seam allowances and the side/bottom piece.

3. Attach the front section in the same way.

Strap

1. Fold and pound 1 inch (2.5 cm) along each long edge.

2. Glue baste to hold the folded edges in place. Topstitch ⅛ inch (3 mm) from each folded edge.

3. Topstitch again ⅛ inch (3 mm) from each raw edge.

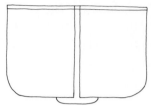

Figure 5.11

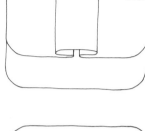

Figure 5.12

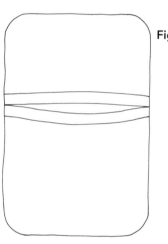

Figure 5.13

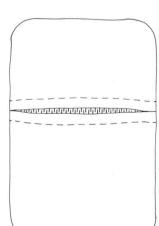

Figure 5.14

An open pocket on the back keeps keys within easy reach.

Lining Pocket

1. Fold down 1 inch (2.5 cm) on the straight edge of one pocket flap. Pound and permanently cement.

2. Lay the wrong side of this piece against the right side of the remaining section, aligning the curved edges. Glue baste. Topstitch ⅛ inch (3 mm) from the folded edge around the curved sides. Stitch again ⅛ inch (3 mm) away.

Lining

1. Center the pocket over the right side of the back lining. Glue baste, upper edges aligned.

2. With right sides together, place the flap lining over the back/pocket section. Apply stay tape over the seamline with glue stick. Stitch through all layers.

3. Finger press the seam allowances open, the pocket allowance toward the flap allowance. Pound and glue baste the seam allowances in place. Topstitch ⅛ inch (3 mm) from each side of the seam.

4. Assemble as for the outer bag, leaving one side seam open to turn right side out after joining the bag to the lining.

Assembling the Bag

1. Place the lining in the bag with right sides together, sandwiching the strap into position between the layers. Make sure the right side of the strap is against the right side of the bag, and have the raw ends extending 3 inches (7.5 cm) beyond the upper seamline. Stitch.

2. Turn Right side out. Finger press and pound, favoring the bag slightly.

3. Topstitch ⅛ inch (3 mm) from the edge around the flap and opening. Topstitch the front flap ¼ inch (7 mm) from the upper zipper stitching line.

It took little extra time to add an elegant deersuede lining to the new bag. A pocket at the upper back holds small essentials.

A larger version of the bag was made, without the flap, of black garment cow and hair-on calf with a stenciled zebra pattern. The stenciling is applied during the processing of the hide.

A small piece of leather stitched over the zipper opening at the tab end reinforces the seam to prolong the life of the zipper.

Hats and Caps

Hats are rewarding projects for beginners and a great way for experienced leather sewers to use up scraps. The cap shown here is made of lightweight pigsuede, an especially suitable material. The crown front of a cap offers a perfect place to display your own machine-embroidered logo or favorite design.

It is not difficult to make your own pattern from a favorite hat. Just remember to add seam allowances. It may be possible to salvage the visor stiffener and adjustment strap for reuse.

A basic cap has extra panache when it's made up of soft pigsuede. To make a personal statement, add a decorative emblem or embroidered design to one of the crown sections before the cap is assembled.

Two-Tone Cap

The visor of this cap is interfaced with a double layer of buckram that was steam shaped over a ham. To construct the visor neatly, we have used the method described on page 72 for collars and pocket flaps.

A narrow seam allowance—¼ inch (7 mm) or so—works best in the crown area. Double topstitching gives a tidy, professional look. A self-covered button adds a great finishing touch; use a glover's needle to sew it in place.

SUPPLIES

- Pigsuede, 1 to 1½ ounce weight at ½ square yard (.5 sq m) total
- Matching thread
- Buckram, ¼ yard (.25 m)
- Bias tape, ⅞ inch (2.25 cm) wide, ⅔ yard (.7 m)
- Elastic, ⅜ inch (1 cm) wide, ⅜ yard (.3 m)
- Button to cover, ⅝ inch (1.5 cm) diameter

CUTTING

1. With the crown pattern piece (figure 5.15), cut six pieces from suede, alternating the colors if you wish.

2. With the visor pattern (figure 5.16), cut two pieces from suede.

3. Cut two visor pieces from buckram, eliminating the seam allowances.

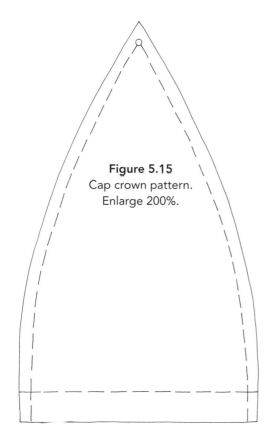

Figure 5.15
Cap crown pattern.
Enlarge 200%.

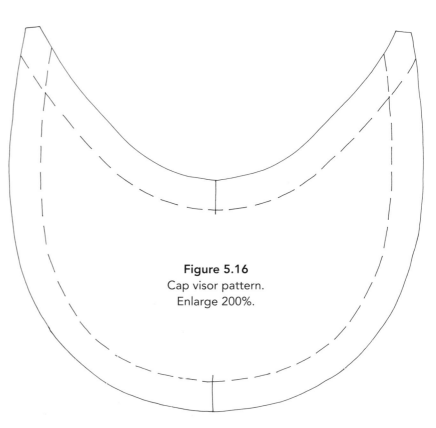

Figure 5.16
Cap visor pattern.
Enlarge 200%.

CONSTRUCTION

1. With right sides together, sew three crown sections together along the curved edges, ending the seams ¼ inch (7 mm) from the points. Tie the thread ends. Topstitch each side of each seam, catching the seam allowance in the stitching.

2. With right sides together, sew the two crown sections together, matching the centers. Finish as in step 1.

3. Place the visor interfacing sections together and steam shape them over a ham. The steam will "glue" them together.

4. Assemble the visor as described on page 72.

5. Sew the visor to the crown, matching centers. Clip the visor seam allowances as necessary.

6. Open one folded edge of the bias tape. Sew to the crown over the visor, placing the bias foldline over the seamline. Turn in ½ inch (1.3 cm) at each end to meet at center back. Slipstitch the ends together.

7. Understitch the bias tape and seam allowances. Turn and pound.

8. For the elastic casing, stitch ½ inch (1.3 cm) from the folded edge 12 inches (30.5 cm) along the crown back.

9. Insert the elastic into the casing. Adjust to fit, and tack the ends.

10. Cover the button and stitch it on top.

CHAPTER 6

Techniques for Garment Making

In Chapter 4 we discussed the basic techniques and stitches that are used for sewing with leather and suede. This section deals with the creation of beautiful, well-constructed garments. Although textiles and leather share many of the same construction techniques—both require interfacings, underlinings, seam stabilizers, and linings—at least some of the time, there are important differences, too. For example, the fact that leather does not ravel opens up a whole new area of design freedom. There are many techniques unique to leather construction that will add a great deal to your finished garments. On pages 124 to 125, you will find pattern information for the garments featured in this chapter.

Leather cording, held in place by loops that are stitched into the lining seam, makes functional and very distinctive buttonholes. The back of the quilted vest is shown on page 111.

Construction Materials

Interfacing, underlining, stay tape, and twill tape are as important in the construction of leather garments as for those made of fabric. Materials should be chosen for compatibility with the leather being used. If the leather is washable, construction materials also should be washable and should be preshrunk before use in same manner the leather is preshrunk. Always, always test fusible material with a scrap of the leather or suede. Lining materials and techniques are discussed in Chapter 7.

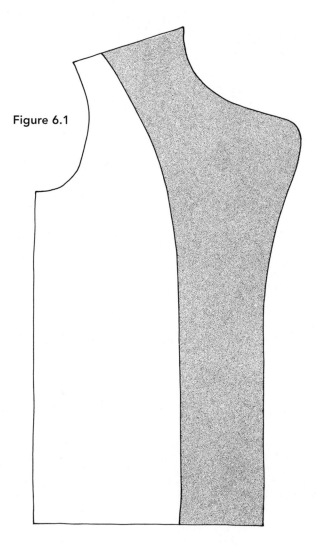

Figure 6.1

INTERFACINGS

Just as it does in garments made of fabric, interfacing in leather garments helps maintain the shape of collars, cuffs, facings, and the like. It also is used to support areas of stress or construction details.

Select interfacing that is compatible with the project and the weight of the skin. Preshrink interfacings according to the manufacturer's instructions. Most of the interfacings used for fabric also are suitable for leather and suede: wovens, nonwovens, and knits, both sew-in and fusible, the latter with special caution and care.

Where to Interface

Use the pattern grainline as a guide for cutting interfacings. Collars, cuffs, waistbands, hems, and front edges are typically interfaced. Jacket fronts can be interfaced just in the chest area (figure 6.1) or entirely. On a jacket or coat, lapels and front edges will have a crisper appearance if a slightly firmer interfacing is used for these areas than for the other interfaced parts of the garment.

Cut interfacing for buttonholes with the least amount of stretch parallel to the opening. If the buttonhole area is already interfaced, apply a small scrap of fusible beneath the buttonhole. To reduce bulk in a waistband, interface only the outside half.

Which Interfacing?

Woven sew-in interfacings that offer soft to firm support are silk and polyester organza, poly/cotton and poly/rayon blends. The same level of support is provided by nonwoven polyester and poly/rayon blends. Sew-in interfacing can be temporarily secured with glue stick or spray-on adhesive.

Fusible interfacings can often be used successfully with leather or suede. There is a wide variety of fusibles available, but the low-temperature types are generally the best choice. Because high iron temperature and steam can damage leather, always test the proposed interfacing on a sample.

Interfacings suitable for leather and suede. Left, top to bottom: very lightweight nonwoven, medium weight nonwoven, organza, woven poly/cotton. Right, top to bottom: fusible hair canvas, woven poly/rayon, weft insertion, fusible tricot, low-temperature fusible.

Test the proposed product on an 8-inch (20 cm) square of the leather or suede you are using. Apply the interfacing with a press cloth according to the manufacturer's instructions. Allow the sample to cool, then check for bonding, shrinkage, color changes, impression lines at the edges, and the finished hand of the sample.

If the sample is satisfactory, proceed with the garment. If not, try another sample with a lower iron temperature setting and less steam or no steam. If the second sample is also unsatisfactory, switch to a sew-in interfacing.

Do not use a Teflon ironing board cover when applying fusibles. It will reflect back heat and moisture. This is not a good thing for hides and skins!

SEAM TAPE

Seam tape serves the same purpose in leather garments as in those made of fabric, stabilizing seams and preventing stretching. Tape can be made of linen, cotton, polyester, or rayon, and is available in both sew-in and fusible forms. Most useful are ½-inch (1.3 cm) and ¼-inch (7 mm) widths. Always preshrink tape according to the manufacturer's instructions.

INTERFACING

As in fabric construction, interfacing helps an area of the garment retain its shape and should be selected to be compatible with the material it is supporting. Many different types of interfacing are suitable including woven, nonwoven, and knit, sewn in and fusible (regular and low temperature). High temperature and steam can damage some leathers. Always test samples before beginning the project.

UNDERLINING

Cut and sewn as one with the individual pieces of a garment, underlining adds body and support. It reduces wrinkling and strengthens thin leather or suede. Underlining is sometimes used as a base for piecing or embellishment on the surface. Lightweight fabric such as Bemberg rayon, lightweight silk, or polyester organza can be used for underlining. Muslin works well when a medium-weight underlining is needed. For a heavy backing, try the polyester-rayon blend often used in men's ties. Many kinds of interfacing serve equally well as underlining.

Construction Techniques

The following garment construction techniques are intended specifically for use with leather. They help shape and finish garments with professional-looking results.

DARTS

In leather, darts that taper gradually toward the point are easier to sew smoothly. Short, wide darts will pucker at the tip, especially in heavier leather. In the latter case, halve the base width of the dart and make two smaller darts for a smoother finish.

Stitch darts from the widest to the narrowest point (photo 1). Tie the thread ends, and add a very small drop of glue to the knot for security. In lightweight leather or suede, small darts may be finger pressed in the appropriate direction and pounded lightly.

For wider darts and those in heavier leather, trim after stitching, leaving a ⅜-inch (1 cm) seam allowance (photo 2). Trim out the small area near the tip, leaving a bit of seam allowance so the stitches will not tear out (photo 3). Finger press open, pound on a seam stick, and cement or topstitch the seam allowances.

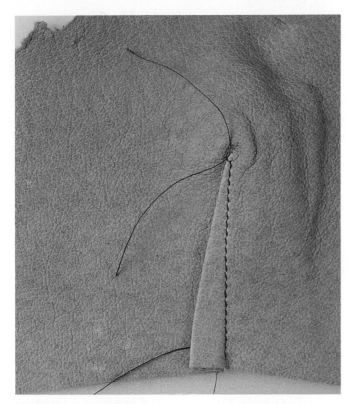

Photo 1

Photo 2

Photo 3

Photo 4. Lapped dart with reinforced point, wrong side

Photo 5. Lapped dart, right side

Photo 6. Slot dart, wrong side

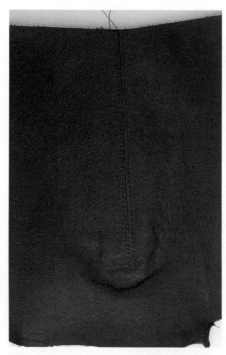

Photo 7. Slot dart, right side

Lapped Dart

Lapped darts are attractive on sporty garments. This technique works well for narrower darts. For wider darts, use the slot method.

For a lapped dart, cut along one dart stitching line to the tip. Using a glue stick, lap the cut edge over the opposite stitching line. Glue baste a small square of interfacing or the leather itself under the dart tip. Topstitch along the cut edge (photos 4 and 5).

For bust darts, cut along the upper stitching line and lap the edge over the lower stitching line. Trim away the excess leather on the wrong side.

Slot Dart

This dart, like the lapped dart, looks good on sportswear. It is a better choice for wide darts and those in heavier leather.

Cut a 1 inch (2.5 cm) strip of the garment leather slightly longer than the dart. Cut the garment section along both dart stitching lines, removing the piece between them. Bring the dart edges together. Glue baste the dart to the strip, carefully abutting the edges of the dart. Topstitch along the dart edges (photos 6 and 7).

HEMS

A hem at the lower edge of a garment or sleeve is cemented or topstitched to secure it. Hems usually do not exceed 2 inches (5 cm) in width.

For a hem on a straight edge, mark the hemline on the wrong side. Turn it up, and pound along the foldline. Open the hem and apply cement to both the garment and the hem to within ½ inch (1.5 cm) of the hem edge. Turn up the hem again and finger press in place. Lift to release tension, then finger press again. Pound, or use a wallpaper roller to press.

A curved hem, such as at the lower edge of a flared skirt, will lie flat if notches are cut from the hem allowance to remove excess fullness prior to cementing. Cut narrow notches so that the cut edges can be abutted to create a smooth hemline, as shown in figure 6.2.

On sporty, unlined garments, the hems can be turned and topstitched in place without cementing. Mark the hem on the wrong side. Glue baste and finger press in place. Topstitch ⅛ inch (3 mm) from the foldline and again ¼ inch (7 mm) from the first stitching. Trim close to the second row of stitching.

For a garment of lightweight leather like lambsuede, you may wish to interface the hem with lightweight fusible interfacing. Then proceed as above.

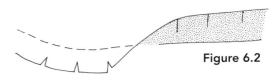

Figure 6.2

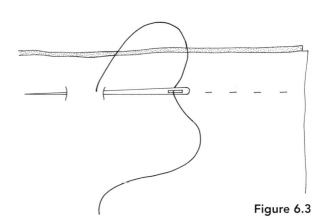

Figure 6.3

ZIPPERS

Zipper application in leather garments is generally the same as for textile garments. There are just a few differences in technique. All zipper types are suitable for use with leather. Even "invisible" zippers can be used with lightweight suede and leather. Select a zipper that is appropriate for the weight of the leather.

The use of a Teflon zipper foot will make zipper application much easier. As an inexpensive alternative, cut adhesive-backed Teflon to size and apply it to the bottom of the standard zipper foot.

To prevent stretching, interface the placket area. Cut interfacing, of an appropriate weight, 1 inch (2.5 cm) longer and wider than the placket area. Follow the manufacturer's instructions for the application of fusibles.

It is not a good idea to use tape to hold the edges of the opening together during zipper application. Adhesive from the tape may leave residue that is difficult or impossible to remove, especially on the surface of suede.

Hand application of a zipper adds a decorative touch to the garment. Use a prickstitch, as shown (figure 6.3). The jacket shown on page 6 features a zipper that was installed this way.

Centered and Lapped Zippers

Follow the package instructions for centered or lapped zipper installation, but do not machine baste the opening. Instead, fold back seam allowances, pound, and secure them with glue stick. Baste the zipper tape in place with double-sided tape or glue stick. Topstitch.

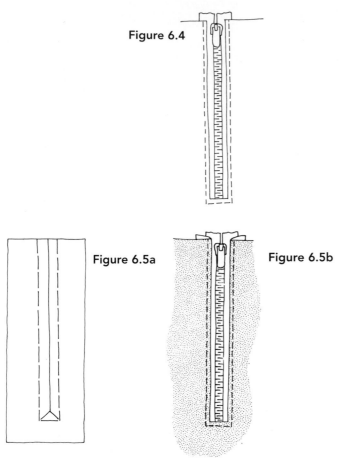

Figure 6.4

Figure 6.5a

Figure 6.5b

Exposed Zippers

Leather garments often feature exposed zippers. This application works equally well in a seam or in a place where there is no seam.

Mark the opening the length of the zipper and wide enough to expose the teeth, approximately ⅜ inch (1 cm). Carefully cut the opening.

Baste the zipper in place with glue stick. Topstitch around the opening (figure 6.4).

A faced opening provides a more polished finish for an exposed zipper, particularly in lighter weight leathers. Cut a rectangular strip of leather approximately 2 inches (5 cm) wider than the proposed opening, and 1 inch (2.5 cm) longer. Place the piece, right sides together, over the marked opening. Stitch around the marked lines. Cut as shown in figure 6.5a. Trim, and turn the facing to the inside. Pound and glue baste the seam allowances, then baste and stitch the zipper as for an exposed zipper without facing (figure 6.5b).

POCKETS

Any pocket style that can be made in fabric also can be made in leather. Figures 6.6–6.14 illustrates some possibilities, and others are shown on the garments throughout the book. For welt pockets, try the bound buttonhole method described on page 82.

When you want two or more identical pockets, or wish to experiment with a shape or size, make a template from lightweight cardboard such as a manila file folder. Stabilize the pocket area by applying interfacing on the garment wrong side. To prevent the pocket opening from stretching, use stay tape at the upper edge of the pocket, securing the ends in the seams.

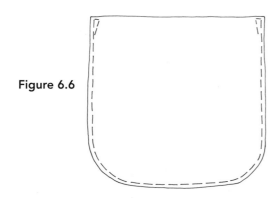

Figure 6.6

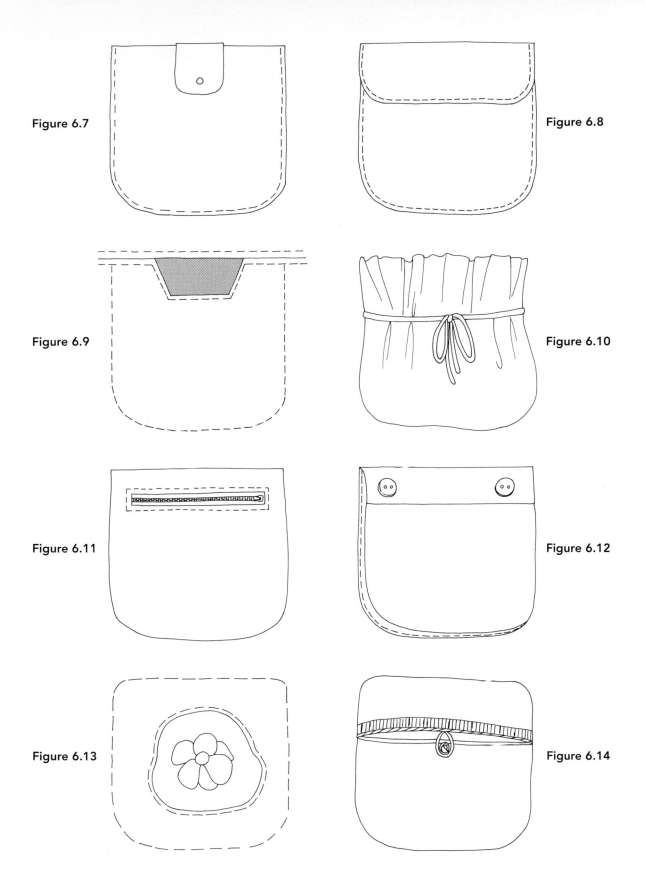

Figure 6.7

Figure 6.8

Figure 6.9

Figure 6.10

Figure 6.11

Figure 6.12

Figure 6.13

Figure 6.14

A traditional shirt is casually elegant in lightweight pigsuede. The collar and pocket flaps were made by the alternative method described here to keep the edges crisp.

COLLARS, CUFFS, AND POCKET FLAPS

Traditional shirt or jacket cuffs, collars, and pocket flaps all are constructed in a similar manner—with an upper section, a facing, and interfacing between the two. These pieces can be made in the same way for leather garments.

Collar points can be difficult to turn. To facilitate turning, sew a few stitches diagonally across the point. As an alternative, round the points slightly.

For all these components, interface the upper section and stitch it, right sides together, to the facing section in the usual manner. Trim and grade the seam allowances. Before turning, pound the seam allowances to deaden them, then finger press and pound the seams open. To secure, turn and topstitch or cement in place.

The following alternative technique produces neatly finished edges on cuffs, flaps, or collars. It is better than the traditional method for medium-weight or heavier leathers especially. This technique also is useful for constructing belts and cap visors. The shirt shown here illustrates a pocket flap made this way.

Cut a template of the pattern piece, without seam allowances, from a manila file folder or similar material. Interface the upper section of the piece. Place the template on the interfaced side. Clip or notch the seam allowance as necessary (figure 6.15).

Turn the seam allowances to the inside, clipping or notching as necessary. Press with a mallet or iron. Remove the template. Glue baste the seam allowances in place, abutting the notched edges (figure 6.16).

With wrong sides together, place upper section on the lower section. The lower section seam allowance extends evenly beyond the turned edges of the upper section. Glue baste. Stitch ⅛ inch (3 mm) inside the folded edge of the upper section and again ¼ inch (7 mm) inside the first row (figure 6.17).

Carefully trim away the extending seam allowance, cutting close to the stitching line (figure 6.18).

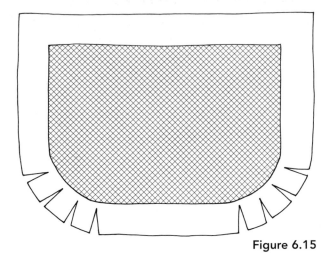

Figure 6.15

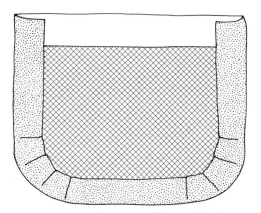

Figure 6.16

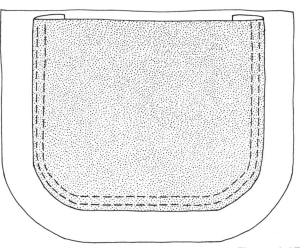

Figure 6.17

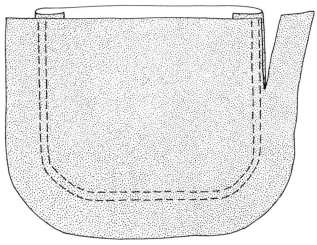

Figure 6.18

The same technique produces a great-looking pointed collar. Begin as for the pocket flap with an interfaced upper collar and a template. Trim diagonally across each point as shown, cutting approximately ¼ to ⅜ inch (.7 to 1 cm) from the point (figure 6.19).

Fold and glue baste the seam allowances as for the pocket flap, trimming away excess seam allowance to produce a flat corner (figure 6.20). Complete as described above.

Another alternative method for reducing bulk in collars, pocket flaps, and cuffs is to use fabric for the facing. Choose a fabric that works with the leather or suede. Interface and stitch as for the traditional method. Use glue stick to secure the leather seam allowance, then topstitch to finish. If the garment design doesn't call for topstitching, understitch the seam allowances to the under collar.

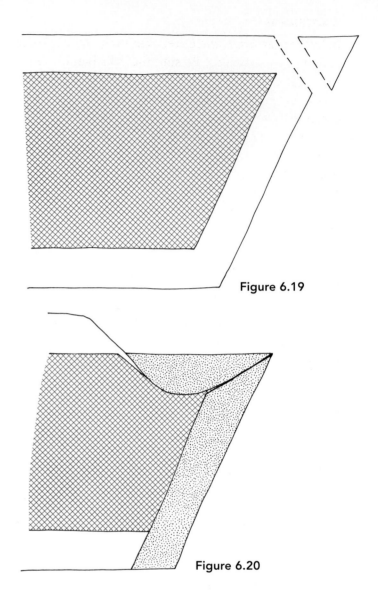

Figure 6.19

Figure 6.20

WAISTBANDS

In leather garments, there are several ways to construct and apply waistbands. Be sure the waistband offered with your garment pattern is compatible with the weight of leather being used. If not, try one of the alternatives described below.

If the garment is to be lined, attach the lining at the waistband seam. Hanger loops can be sewn into the seam at the same time. Interface the band with an interfacing appropriate for the weight of the leather. Premade waistband interfacing, fusible or sew-in, is available in standard band widths. Some incorporate a desirable non-roll feature. Use an additional small piece of interfacing to reinforce the area where hooks or buttons will be placed.

Topstitching is often used as a design detail on waistbands. Make sure the stitching is compatible with, or repeats, topstitching on other areas of the garment. Lengthen the stitch a bit to make topstitching more pronounced.

Tailored Waistbands

A traditional waistband, like that shown on page 81, is used on most tailored garments. The pattern usually will have an overlapping end that is flush with the edge of the zipper placket. A buttonhole or hook is sewn at this end. The other end, generally the left side on women's garments, usually is extended by approximately 1½ inches (4 cm). Buttons or hook loops are set on this underlay extension.

To construct this waistband, check that the pattern allows for a flush overlap and an extended underlay as described above and adjust if necessary. Apply an appropriate interfacing, with an extra layer when hooks are to be used. If standard interfacing is used, eliminate seam allowances and glue baste in place. Avoid glue in the seam allowance areas.

Fold the band in half lengthwise, right sides together. Stitch the overlap end. For the underlay end, stitch across the end and stitch the portion of the long edges that will form the extension.

A classic Miyaki skirt pattern is made up in lightweight pigsuede. The wrapped style features a dropped front panel attached to the dropped rear belt with antique glass buttons.

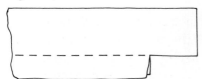

Figure 6.21

Trim, grade, and skive the seam allowances. Finger press the seam open and tap with a mallet over a point press. Turn the band right side out. Tap with a mallet to press. Clip the inside seam allowances of the extension (figure 6.21).

Apply the waistband to the skirt or pants along with the lining. First, assemble and press the lining, then place it in the garment with wrong sides together. With right sides together, stitch the waistband to the garment. Trim, grade, and skive the seam allowances. Finger press the band in place, seam allowances toward the band, and tap with a mallet.

The remaining inner waistband seam allowance extends below the waistband stitching line. Align the seamlines and glue baste—in the waistband area, not in the seam allowance—to keep the band in place.

From the right side, stitch in the ditch through all layers. Trim the inner seam allowance and interfacing close to the stitching line.

Faced Waistbands

With heavy or bulky leather it is best to make the band in two parts, using leather for the outer half and making a facing of grosgrain ribbon or fabric. Both variations are constructed essentially in the same way. Cut the outer leather portion of the band the finished band width and length plus seam allowances all around.

To face a band with grosgrain ribbon, use a piece of ribbon the finished width of the band. The length should equal the waistband length plus two seam allowances. Interface the leather section. Lap one long edge of the ribbon over the upper stitching line of the leather band section, ribbon wrong side against the leather right side. Glue baste, and stitch close to the ribbon edge. Fold with wrong sides together. Finger press and tap with a mallet to press along the foldline, making sure the ribbon is not visible from the band right side.

To finish the ends, fold the piece lengthwise with right sides together. Stitch each end. Trim, grade, and turn. Press with a mallet.

Apply the waistband to the garment with right sides together. Trim and grade seam allowances. If a hook and eye closure will be used, sew the hook to the ribbon side of the waistband. Trim, grade, and pound the seam allowances toward the band. Trim away the seam allowance along the extension.

Topstitch around all edges, catching the ribbon edge. If topstitching does not fit the design plan, whipstitch the free edge of the ribbon to the waistband seam, turning under or trimming away the seam allowance in the extension area.

A waistband faced with fabric is constructed in the same way as one with a grosgrain facing. Interface the fabric as necessary. Prior to stitching the band, finish the lower long edge with bias binding.

Faced Waistline

A third type of waist treatment eliminates the waistband altogether, and instead features a shaped facing that is cut using the garment pattern as a guide. Use the same leather if it is light in weight, otherwise use a lighter leather or suede, or textile.

To create the facing, fold out any darts or pleats on the pattern front and back pieces. Cut facing pieces approximately 2 to 3 inches (5 to 7.5 cm) wide, plus seam allowance. Interface the sections if necessary. Stitch together at the sides to form one piece. Finish the lower edge as desired. Bias binding made of lining fabric is a good choice for leather and suede; it provides a fabric edge that can be hand sewn to the lining for a more professional look.

Position the finished lining in the garment, wrong sides together. Glue baste around the upper edge.

To keep the waistline from stretching, glue baste narrow stay tape over the seamline on the facing wrong side. With right sides together, stitch the facing to garment at the waistline. Finger press the seam allowances toward the facing. Tap with a mallet. Understitch through the facing and seam allowances close to the waist seam so the facing will not roll outward.

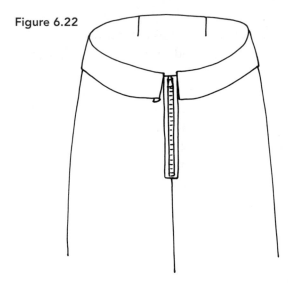

Figure 6.22

Turn the facing to the inside of the garment, rolling the seam slightly to the inside. Pound with mallet to press. Facing ends can be turned back and hand tacked along the zipper. In heavier leather, trim away the seam allowances and topstitch along the zipper stitching lines (figure 6.22).

Waist Finish for Heavy Leather

If the garment leather is very heavy, eliminate the band or facing altogether. First, stitch the vertical seams in the garment and finish them as desired. Install the zipper. On the wrong side of the garment, glue baste narrow twill tape over the waist seamline.

Stitch the vertical seams in the lining. Fold under the seam allowances along the zipper opening and insert the lining in the garment with right sides together. Stitch the lining to the garment around the waist. Turn, pound, and edgestitch through the lining and seam allowances, or topstitch through all layers. Hand tack the lining to the zipper tape. Add a hook and eye at the upper end of the zipper.

Elastic Waists

Very soft, loose pants or skirts of lamb or pigsuede are most comfortable with an elastic waistband. Most garment patterns can be adapted for elastic waistbands if there is enough ease to fit over the hips. Elastic 1 inch (2.5 cm) wide is comfortable for most people, but wider elastic or multiple rows of narrow elastic will work as well.

The following method describes installation of a finished lining as part of the elastic waistband application. Cut a waistband of suede or leather that is two times the width of the elastic, plus ¼-inch (7 mm) ease, plus two seam allowances. The length is the waist measurement of the garment, plus two seam allowances. The total waist measurement must have enough ease that the band will fit comfortably over the hips.

Sew the short ends together, leaving an opening on the inner side of the band that is wide enough for the elastic to pass through easily. This opening will be placed at the inside center back.

Finish the lining and attach it to the long edge of the waistband, the side with the opening. Press the seam allowances toward the lining. Apply waistband to the garment with right sides together. Wrap the waistband around these seam allowances to form a casing for the elastic. From the garment right side, stitch in the ditch. Install the elastic and whipstitch the opening closed.

PIPING, BINDING, AND CORDING

Piping, binding, and cording are grouped together as finishing techniques. While different in execution, all serve to bind edges or are used to create closures in a way that completes the design.

Piping

Piping gives crisp definition at garment edges. It can blend with the garment, or add contrast. Try using smooth leather piping with suede, or suede with smooth leather. The textural difference adds interest even when the colors are similar. Piping is usually filled with cord, but this is not always necessary with leather, especially if the leather is substantial.

Cut the piping strip a bit longer than the length of the edge or seam to be trimmed. If piecing is necessary, join strips with diagonal seams to reduce bulk. In width, the strips should measure two seam allowances, plus the circumference measurement of the cord being covered.

For corded piping, wrap the strip around the cord, right side out. Sew with a zipper foot and lengthened stitch near, but not exactly next to, the cord. Position the

Figure 6.23a

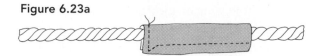

Figure 6.23b

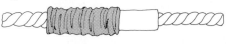

piping on the right side of the garment. With a regular stitch length sew the piping exactly next to the cording, inside the first stitching line. Clip or notch seam allowances to fit the piping smoothly around curves and corners.

Remove the cord from the end of the piping to reduce bulk. To further reduce bulk, angle the piping into the seam a bit before the seam end. Continue with construction. Use the previous seamline as a stitching guide.

Lightweight pigsuede makes attractive narrow piping to trim a plonge vest. Brocade fabric used for the collar band facing and button coverings adds color and texture. Slot buttonholes are incorporated into a faced shape, also of pigsuede.

Cording

Covered cording is similar to piping, but with the seam allowances turned to the inside. It is used to make ties, button loops, and decorative knots. Lighter weight leathers are the best choice for cording.

To make covered cording, cut leather or suede strips the circumference of the filler cord plus two seam allowances. Piece strips diagonally to the required length.

Purchase filler cord twice the needed length. Mark the length of the leather strip on the filler cord, measuring from one end. Do not cut. Wrap the strip, wrong side out, around the "second length" of the cord, beginning at the mark. Secure it with binder clips.

With a zipper foot, stitch across the cord to secure the end, then turn, stitching a funnel shape at the turn, and stitch the length of the cord (figure 6.23a). Stitching the funnel makes it a bit easier to evert the cord.

Trim the corner and seam allowances. Slide the fabric over the cording, turning it to the right side at the same time (figure 6.23b). Cut the filler cord near the sewn end.

Binding

Because it eliminates the need for facings, binding is often the least bulky way to finish a garment. It also is a great way to join bulky handwoven fabrics.

Leather has no true grain, so binding strips can be cut in any direction. For binding with a finished width of ½ inch (1.3 cm) and ⅝ inch (1.5 cm) seam allowances, cut strips 2½ inches (6.5 cm) wide to allow for the turn of the "cloth." Where piecing is necessary, join the strips with diagonal seams.

Clip the binding to the garment edge with right sides together and raw edges aligned. Stitch, trim the seam allowances to ⅜ inch (1 cm) and grade them (photo 8). Wrap the strip around the raw edge. Stitch in the ditch from the right side (photos 9 and 10). On the back, trim close to the stitching and tap with a mallet to press.

Cording offers an innovative alternative to standard buttonholes. Stuffed cording slips through tabs sewn into the front vest/lining seam and accommodates buttons of several sizes.

Photo 8

Photo 9
Wrong side.

Photo 10
Right side.

It is helpful to stretch the center of the binding strip when going around outside curves. Notch out the seam allowance to reduce bulk. Another tip for fitting around outer curves is to sew a line of gathering stitches close to the binding outside edge and draw it up to fit.

On inside curves, stretch the seam and seam allowance a bit. This gives just a bit more ease and the garment will hang smoothly.

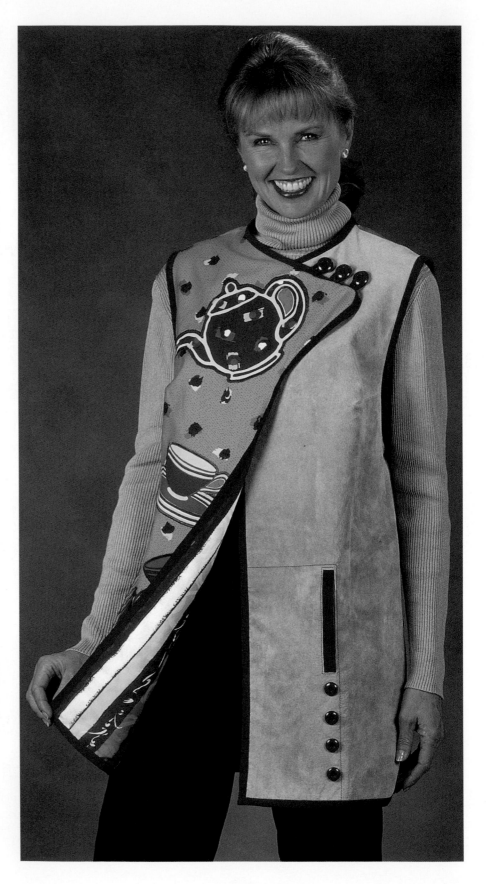

Edge bindings, button loops, and welt pocket, all in crimson pigsuede, give special definition to an elongated vest. For the vest itself, lightweight pigsuede on the one side complements the whimsical cotton print used for the other.

Bound Seams

Leather binding provides a clever means of joining bulky fabrics. Each side of the seam to be joined is bound, then the bindings themselves are joined.

Begin by removing seam allowances from the seams to be bound. Stitch a leather binding strip to each fabric edge with right sides together and the raw edges aligned. Trim and grade the seam allowances. Place bindings right sides together and sew (photo 11). Finger press the seam open, glue baste the seam allowances in place, and stitch in the ditch from the right side (photo 12). On the wrong side, trim close to the stitching.

Photo 11   Photo 12

BUTTONHOLES

There are a number of ways to make buttonholes in leather and suede garments. Since it is not necessary to overcast raw edges, many buttonhole variations are possible with leather and suede that wouldn't work with fabric. For alternatives to traditional buttonholes, see Faced Shapes for Buttonholes and Pockets, pages 104 to 105.

To prevent the buttonholes stretching out of shape, it is a good idea to reinforce behind each one. Use an additional small piece of interfacing.

Because leather doesn't ravel, buttonhole edges need not be overcast. This buttonhole, on the waistband of traditionally styled washable leather pants, is especially suited to leather and suede and is quick and easy to apply.

Simple Buttonhole

The quickest way to make a buttonhole is to stitch a single or double rectangle around the marked buttonhole, then slash along the marked line. If there is a facing, as at the front edge of a jacket, cement the facing in place and sew through both the garment and the facing. Cut the opening with a buttonhole chisel, sharp craft knife, or single-edged razor blade.

Machine Buttonholes

Machine buttonholes usually can be worked on leather and suede. Lengthen the stitch a bit to prevent perforating the leather. If skipped stitches are a problem, use a piece of tear-away stabilizer behind the buttonhole. Color the raw edges with a matching permanent marking pen to mask the interfacing and stabilizer.

Corded machine buttonholes are attractive. Follow the instructions in your machine manual.

Bound Buttonholes

Bound buttonholes are good looking in leather garments. Traditional bound buttonhole techniques will work, but this modified version is less bulky. If the leather is thin, make the lips rather narrow. With heavier leather, make wider lips.

For multiple buttonholes that are identical and spaced evenly from the garment edge, use a template cut from lightweight cardboard such as a manila file folder. The following instructions will accommodate an opening up to ½ inch (1.3 cm) wide.

Cut a rectangular hole in the template the exact size of the finished buttonhole opening. Place the opening in the template the same distance from the template edge as the buttonholes will be from the garment edge.

Mark the openings on the garment front. Keeping the facing free, cut the openings with a buttonhole chisel, sharp craft knife, or single-edged razor blade.

To form the lips, cut two leather strips 1 inch (2.5 cm) wide and 1 inch (2.5 cm) longer than the finished length of the buttonhole. Spread permanent cement on the wrong side of each strip, fold it in half lengthwise, and tap with a mallet. Roll with a wallpaper roller. To stabilize stretchy leather, place narrow stay tape along the foldline,

then cement. For multiple buttonholes, cut and cement long strips, then cut to the needed length.

Abut the folded edges of two strips at the center of each buttonhole opening. Glue baste in place.

Position the facing and glue baste. From the garment right side, stitch around the buttonhole close to the edges of the opening. On the facing side, cut away the area inside the stitching.

In-seam Buttonholes

An in-seam buttonhole is simply a finished opening within a seam. Interface the area of the seamline that will become the buttonhole. Mark the buttonhole. Stitch the seam, interrupting the stitching between the markings. Leave long thread tails and tie them off in a square knot. Finger press the seam open and tap with a mallet. If there is a facing or lining, make the opening the same way and cement or stitch in place by hand or machine.

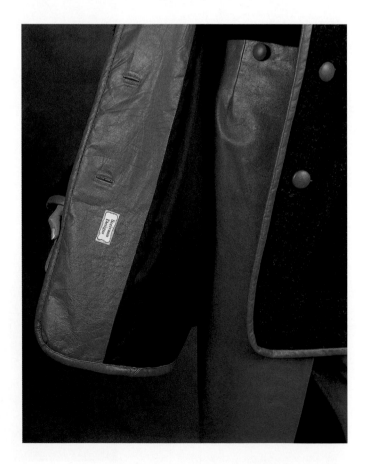

Lightweight cowhide is used for binding, buttons, and buttonhole welts on a bulky mohair coat. In leather, it is a simple matter to give the buttonholes a neat appearance on the facing side. Note that the edge of the facing is bound with lining fabric for an elegant finish. Because of the fabric thickness, the shoulder seams were joined according to the method described on page 81.

BUTTONS AND OTHER CLOSURES

In leather garments, functional buttons must be supported with reinforcing buttons. These reduce stress on the outer buttons and prevent tearing the leather. Reinforcing buttons are small, flat buttons with the same number of holes as the outer buttons. Sew them inside the garment, directly under each outer button, creating a shank if necessary.

Choose buttons that are strong enough and have enough visual weight to support the garment. Select buttons that are durable. Leather garments have a long life span, so pick buttons that will last, such as horn.

Self-covered buttons can be made at home with a kit, or an upholstery shop often will make them for a small charge. Consider adding some stitching or stenciling to the leather before making the button. Thin leather or suede is best for use with home kits.

Chinese Knot Buttons

Traditional knots combine well with leather loops or cording. Make the knots of narrow leather lacing strips or with leather cording, either of which can be made or purchased.

The size of the tubing is proportionate to the size of the button. For example, ³⁄₁₆-inch (5 mm) tubing makes a button ³⁄₈ inch (1 cm) in diameter; ³⁄₈-inch (1 cm) tubing makes a button approximately 1 inch (2.5 cm) across.

To cut a continuous leather lacing strip, begin with a circle of the garment leather. Cut from the outer edge toward the center of the circle in a spiral. Keep the width even for best results.

Experiment to find the length of cord or strip you will need for a knot. Loop the strip as shown (figure 6.24). Loop under the first loop, then over the end. Take care to avoid twisting the leather as the loops are formed (figure 6.25).

Loop a third time, weaving through the two previous loops (figure 6.26). Tighten the loops, easing the piece into a ball shape. Trim the ends and cement or sew them flat on the underside of the button. Attach the button to the garment with a thread shank or a hook eye sewn onto the bottom (figure 6.27).

Toggle Buttons

Buttons of rolled leather shapes are a designer touch worth trying. An elongated leather triangle will produce graduated stair-step edges on a barrel button. Rectangles can be rolled into cylinders. The length of the shape and the thickness of the leather determine the diameter of the button.

To make a barrel button, begin with a triangle approximately 3 inches (7.5 cm) long and 1 inch (2.5 cm) wide at the base. Close to the narrow end, punch two small holes approximately ¼ inch (.5 cm) apart at the center of the piece.

Roll the triangle tightly from the wide to the narrow end. Mark through the holes onto the next-to-last layer. Cut slits across at the marked positions for insertion of the tip (figure 6.28).

Unroll the piece. Run a thin line of permanent cement down the center of the triangle, stopping short of the small holes at the tip. Reroll the piece tightly, inserting the tip through the slits (figure 6.29). Sew through the holes to attach the button.

Snaps

Snaps, too, can be used on leather garments and are available in a range of decorative styles. Choose snaps that are appropriate for the garment design and the weight of the leather. Follow the manufacturer's instructions for application. A scrap of interfacing behind each snap section will reinforce the leather and help prevent the snap from pulling out.

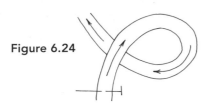

Figure 6.24

Figure 6.25

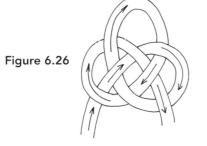

Figure 6.26

Figure 6.27

The shaped face of black pigsuede features slot buttonholes for the silk brocade buttons to slip through. The black suede continues as piping to complete the design.

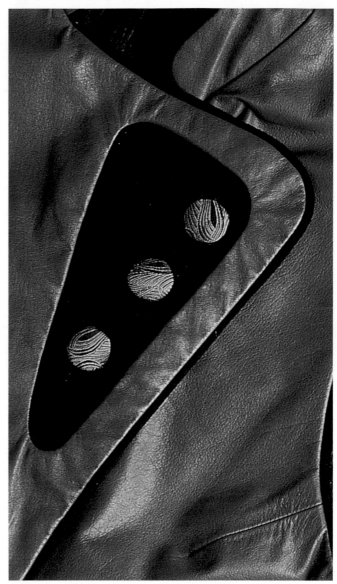

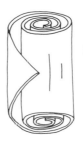

Figure 6.28

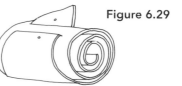

Figure 6.29

CHAPTER 7

Making a Leather Garment

Successful garments of leather and suede require careful planning and cutting, as will be discussed in this chapter. With these considerations, your garment will have the beauty and longevity characteristic of the material. Good planning, combined with the correct construction techniques described in Chapters 4 and 6 and interesting embellishment ideas discussed in Chapter 8, will produce smashing results. You will create a garment that is both visually arresting and technically superior. On pages 124 to 125, you will find pattern information for the garments featured in this chapter.

Distressed lamb, artistically pieced, creates a tunic vest that's simply spectacular. The silk lining was encouraged to roll outward slightly at the edges, then topstitched in place to simulate a piped effect. Use leathers of the same weight for best results when piecing a garment, or interface the thinner pieces so all will be similar.

Choosing a Pattern

Almost anything that can be made of fabric can be made of leather as well. Because leather and suede are beautiful materials, the simplest designs often are the most effective. A garment with classic lines will have the longest fashion life. Leather is very durable, so consider a design that will look stylish for several years. Choose a style that is flattering to you, and that is within your sewing capability.

PIECING A PATTERN

Patterns with fewer pieces are easier to construct, but because few skins and hides are large enough to accommodate full-sized pattern pieces needed for long or voluminous garments, piecing often is necessary. Piecing seams can be incorporated into the garment design very effectively (figures 7.1–7.8).

Draw the new piecing seamlines on the pattern pieces. Make a copy of each new section, adding a seam allowance to each side of each new seam. Avoid piecing near major construction seams as this will create too much bulk and can weaken the garment.

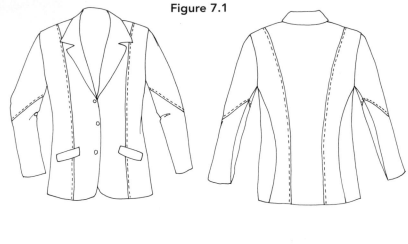

Figure 7.1

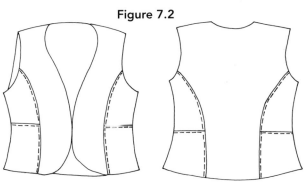

Figure 7.2

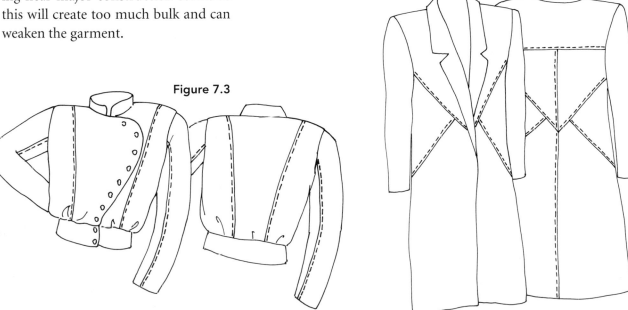

Figure 7.3

Figure 7.4

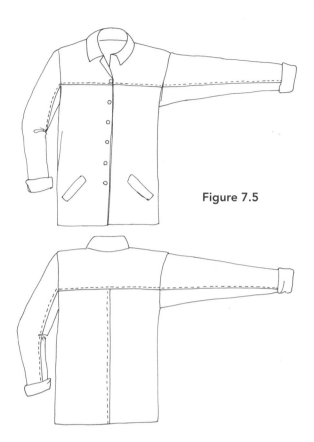

Figure 7.5

Figure 7.6

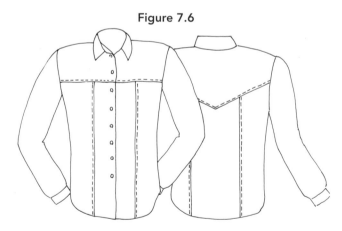

Black pigsuede with wool/silk makes an elegant tunic. The wool and silk skirt fabric adds just the right note as a trim. The pocket offers a chance to explore imaginative fabric and leather combinations, taking advantages of the leather's irregular edges in the design.

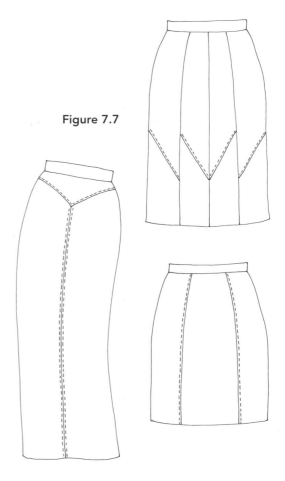

Figure 7.7

Figure 7.8

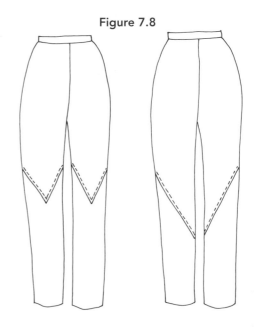

Technically it's not pieced, but a skirt pattern like this one, made up of multiple panels, is a good choice for leather because it reduces waste. Luscious pigsuede provides a perfect background to display the handmade silver buttons.

PREPARING THE PATTERN

Seam allowances on most patterns are ⅝ inch (1.5 cm). In leather construction, ⅜ to ½ inch (1 to 1.3 cm) seam allowance is the standard, except where there will be topstitching more than ¼ inch (.7 cm) from the seamline. Whatever seam allowance you use, be sure to be consistent throughout the pattern.

With leather and suede, garment pieces are always cut from a single thickness. Pattern pieces designated to be cut on the fold must be redrawn as full-sized pieces. For pieces marked "cut two," make a copy of the piece and label them "left" and "right." Remember to turn one of the pieces over before marking. Forgetting this step results in two pieces for one side and none for the other.

FITTING THE PATTERN

Before cutting into the leather, take time to fit the pattern and make all necessary adjustments. Don't be tempted to skip this step! It is a very good idea to make a test garment of muslin, nonwoven pattern-drafting material, denim, or felt that is similar in weight to your leather. Note necessary adjustments on the test garment, then transfer the markings to the pattern pieces.

Leather conforms to the body as it is worn. To accommodate this characteristic, increase sleeve length ½ to 1 inch (1.5 to 2.5 cm) and pant length 1 to 2 inches (2.5 to 5 cm). For close-fitting pants and skirts, cut according to the actual hip measurement without adding ease; the garment will stretch the first time it is worn.

Most leather garments are lined according to the traditional methods. Lining for close-fitting garments should be cut with the usual amount of ease, as lining fabric does not stretch. Cut pant and skirt lining at least 1 inch (2.5 cm) shorter than the finished pant or skirt length.

Leather does not ease well, especially the heavier weights. Consider this when choosing a pattern. The amount of ease may need to be reduced, particularly in the sleeve cap.

Pattern Layout

Careful layout is very important when working with leather and suede. A little extra care at taken this stage will assure a beautiful garment and help prevent expensive mistakes.

GRAINLINES

Fabric is made by weaving fixed warp (lengthwise) fibers at right angles to weft (crosswise) fibers. Grain is the direction the fiber runs—lengthwise or crosswise. Bias is any diagonal that intersects these two grainlines (figure 7.9).

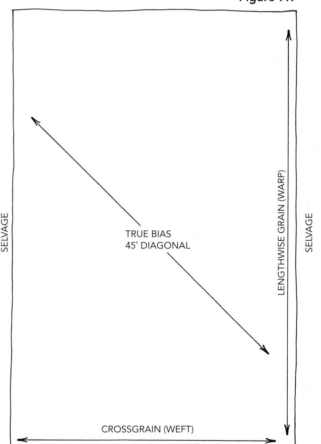

Figure 7.9

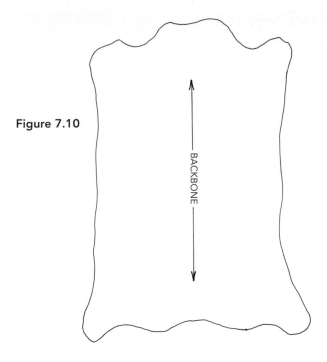

Figure 7.10

BACKBONE

Each of the grainlines has certain characteristics that affect the way a garment will hang or drape. Most often the lengthwise grain runs vertically on a garment because fabric has little or no stretch in this direction. Crosswise grain is placed horizontally around the body because fabric has greater capacity for stretch in this direction, making the garment more comfortable to wear.

Fabric stretches most along the bias, a quality utilized to achieve soft drape in a garment.

Leather is formed by fibers twisting and wrapping around each other and has no true grainlines in the same sense as fabric has; however, garments cut with the pattern grainlines parallel to the backbone of the animal will hang better. If the garment is being cut from leather with the natural grain left intact (top grain leather), it will be more attractive if laid out with direction in mind (figure 7.10).

Pattern pieces can be laid out top to bottom or end to end without losing the directional characteristic. It is best not to cut major pattern pieces in the crosswise direction. Smaller, less noticeable pieces can be cut this direction.

Lay out the pattern pieces with the hide or skin right side up. The advantage of right-side-up placement is a visible surface. Desirable characteristics in grain and color are apparent. Flaws can be seen and avoided. Hold the leather up to the light. Unnoticed holes will become apparent.

The back and shoulder areas of a hide are strongest. Use these areas to cut pieces that will be subject to wearing stress: the seat of pants or a skirt, knees in pants, and the outer sleeve of a jacket or coat. In addition, match the thickness of the hide in related areas of the garment. For example, do not cut one sleeve from a thin area of the hide and the other from a thick area. When cutting the major garment pieces, avoid the outer edges of the hide too; the leather in those areas is more elastic. Distribute thick and thin spots evenly. Reinforce any thin places with interfacing.

PATTERNED SKINS

With embossed or exotic hides or skins, consider the pattern or markings when you plan a cutting layout. Natural markings add a strong design element. Pattern markings can be matched or arranged in unusual ways to create visual impact.

Use the best-matched, most attractive pieces of the skin for the most noticeable parts of the garment, such as jacket fronts and sleeve fronts. If possible, cut adjoining pieces from the same hide to create a more uniform appearance.

LAYOUT FOR NAPPED SKINS

Sueded skins usually have a nap that runs from the neck of the animal toward the tail, and from the backbone outward toward the legs. Pattern pieces should be laid out in the same direction, with the top of each pattern piece toward the neck edge of the skin. To help make the most economical use of a skin, be aware that pattern pieces can usually be shifted up to 25 percent without affecting a satisfactory napped layout.

Some sueded skins do not have a noticeable nap. If your fingers do not leave tracks in one direction as you run them along the surface of the skin, a napped layout is unnecessary.

Start with a pair of jeans, green pigsuede, and cheerful cotton gingham for a jacket that has plenty of pizzazz.

The jacket back features piped and pieced strips, embellished with a collection of faceted glass buttons.

BEFORE YOU CUT

Now it's time to *think, think, think*! Before you cut, check each point on the list below. Take a short break, come back, and *recheck* the list.

LEATHER-CUTTING CHECKLIST

✔ Are all pattern adjustments made and marked, including seam allowance changes and additions?

✔ Have "cut-on-the-fold" pattern pieces been redrawn as single full-sized pieces?

✔ Have "cut two" pattern pieces been duplicated and correctly marked as to left and right?

✔ Have piecing decisions been made and seam allowances added to the new seamlines?

✔ With suede, has the nap been established and all the pieces laid out in the same direction?

✔ Have imperfections in the skin been marked?

✔ Are major pattern pieces laid out parallel to the backbone with the best areas reserved for the front and sleeves?

✔ Have thin spots been reinforced, if necessary?

Cutting Out

Use a rotary cutter and mat for the most efficient cutting. Very sharp shears are an alternative. If your pattern weights are spiked, turn them over to avoid damage to the leather. Cut with long, even strokes to avoid jagged edges on the leather.

MARKING CONSTRUCTION DETAILS

Many of the traditional means of marking construction details on garment pieces are not appropriate for leather and suede. Some leave visible marks on the right side of the leather; some can damage the material.

Mark notches and match points with a ⅛ inch (3 mm) snip in the center of the notch. Darts, foldlines, center front lines, and other details can be marked on the reverse side of the leather with a Hera marker, chalk marker, fine tipped permanent marker, ballpoint pen, or soap sliver with sharpened edges. Always test on a scrap to make sure the marking does not show on the right side.

With a Hera marker, follow the marking lines with moderate pressure, using a ruler as a guide for straight lines. With other marking methods, lift and fold back the pattern along the line to be marked. Use a ruler as a guide to mark the line.

With some leathers there is little difference in appearance between the right and wrong sides. Label the wrong side of each piece to avoid confusion.

Keep the cut pieces flat. If the garment won't be sewn right away, roll the pieces onto a cardboard tube such as those from home decorator fabrics. Wrap the roll in plain brown kraft paper—not plastic—and store it away from direct light and heat.

Lining Leather Garments

Just like garments made of fabric, leather garments are usually lined to cover construction details, increase wearing comfort, and aid shape retention. Lining can prolong the life of the garment. In leather garments, lining also prevents crocking of color onto skin or garments worn underneath. Tailored garments and those with considerable construction detail always should be lined. Soft, loose-fitting garments of lighter weight suede or leather may not need linings.

Smooth, tightly woven fabric usually is the best choice for lining, as it slips more easily over skin and other garments. Qualities to look for in lining fabrics are strength, breathability, and wrinkle resistance. Sometimes cotton flannel or quilted cotton is used to line the body of a garment, but the sleeves should be lined with a slippery fabric for wearing ease.

Since leather has such a long life, it is not unusual for the lining to wear out before the garment does. Choose a sturdy, high-quality material—such as twill—that will wear well. Traditional lining fabrics include Bemberg rayon, many silk fabrics (China silk is rather fragile and should not be used with leather), many kinds of polyester, and several types of acetate. Match the weight of the lining to that of the leather being used, and be sure the lining has the same care requirements as the leather. With washable leather, choose washable material for lining.

Lining can play an important part in the overall garment design. Lining fabric in a complementary color, texture, or pattern becomes a decorative element as well as serving a practical purpose.

LINING SKIRTS AND PANTS

Lining in pants and skirts is usually attached at the waistline seam as the band is applied. It is hand tacked in place around the zipper. The lining hem(s) generally hang free and are finished at least 1 inch (2.5 cm) shorter than the hemmed garment. With some garment styles a partial lining can be used.

Experiment with fabrics beyond the traditional linings. Patterned lightweight silk, silk or polyester charmeuse, contrasting colors and prints all can lend an interesting element to a leather garment design.

Overlapping layers of lamb and pigsuede top a jacket made of black garment cow. French knots secure the layers (a close-up is shown on page 103), and the zipper is handpicked.

Attached Skirt Lining Hem

For a couture finish to skirts, the lining hem can be attached. The effect is easy to accomplish.

Begin by sewing the lengthwise seams and design details on the garment, such as darts, pockets, or pleats. Sew or iron narrow stay tape to the wrong side of the waist seamline.

Mark and hem the skirt with stitching or permanent contact cement, but leave approximately 1 inch (2.5 cm) free at the inner raw edge so the lining can be attached by machine. The shell of the garment is now finished except for the waistband.

Complete the lengthwise seams on the lining. Leave the zipper area open, as it will be attached by hand later. Mark the hemline. Leave a seam allowance below the marked line and cut away the remainder.

With right sides together, sew the lining to the skirt at the hem, lightly glue basting the seam allowances. This prevent the lining fabric from slipping during stitching. Lengthen the stitch slightly to duplicate the look of a hand-sewn seam. Stitch, with the leather on the bottom. Pull the lining up into the skirt, matching waistlines. Glue baste in the seam allowance. Complete the garment by applying the waistband and hand tacking the lining to the zipper tape.

COAT AND JACKET LININGS

Jackets and coats are always lined. A jacket usually has a closed hem. On coats, the hem is most often free, the lining attached to the garment with French tacks to keep the two together.

Bagged Lining

An industry technique known as "bagging" provides an efficient means of applying a lining almost entirely by machine. To begin, complete the outer shell of the garment, including facings. Tack the shoulder pads in place. Hem the sleeves and lower edge, leaving approximately ¾ to 1 inch (2 to 2.5 cm) free at each edge to attach the lining.

Add a center back seam to the lining if the pattern does not include one. Assemble the body of the lining, leaving the center portion of the center back seam open (figure 7.11).

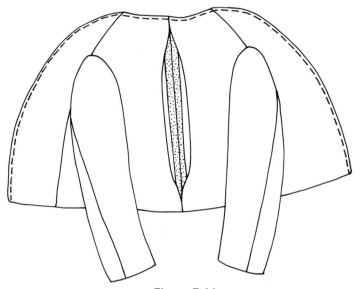

Figure 7.11

With right sides together, clip the lining to the jacket around the neck and front facings. For a designer accent, incorporate narrow piping into this seam. Glue baste lightly in the seam allowances to prevent slipping during stitching.

Stitch around the entire facing and neckline, beginning and ending 1 inch (2.5 cm) short of the hemline on each side. Press the seam toward the lining and permanently cement the facings to the jacket, or catch stitch the edges of the facings to the underlining. Turn the jacket right side out.

Insert the sleeve linings into the sleeves, wrong sides together. Match the seamlines, and make sure the linings are not twisted. Clip the hem edges of the sleeves to the sleeve linings to hold them in place. Reach into the jacket through the open hem at the lower edge and pull out the sleeves, turning them wrong side out. Re-clip the sleeve and sleeve lining edges with right sides together. Stitch, easing the lining if necessary. Turn the sleeves right side out and smooth the lining in place. Tack the lining to the garment at the underarms and shoulder points.

Lining can work as a design element in addition to being functional, especially when the garment is lined to the edges. A good quality fabric was chosen for this jacket lining and the matching shell, the color matching the lambskin piping at the jacket edge and the accent leather on the peplum.

The unfinished lining length should be approximately ¾ inch (2 cm) longer than the finished jacket hemline. Trim away any excess from the lining edge. Reach through the center back lining opening and pull through the lining and garment hems. With right sides together, match and clip together the lining and jacket hem edges. Stitch from facing to facing. It will not be possible to machine stitch all the way to the ends of the seam. Hand tack the last few inches, easing the lining to fit.

Turn the hem back through the center back opening and smooth it in place. Slipstitch the opening.

Removable Lining

A lining variation permits a change from insulated or fur lining in cold weather to twill for the milder seasons. Finish the neck and front facing edges with snap tape, applying the socket side to the garment and the ball side to the lining. Finish the garment and lining hems separately at the lower edge and sleeves. Secure the lining to the garment with buttons and loops at the underarms and sleeve hems. Leave the lower hems free.

Zip-In Lining

Separating zippers that can be cut to length are available in several basic colors. Follow the manufacturer's directions for installation of the slide and stops.

To apply the zipper, assemble the garment facings and remove the seam allowance along the lining edge. Bind this edge with lightweight bias binding. Place the zipper face up under the bound edge with the bound edge extending approximately ¼ inch (7 mm) beyond the zipper teeth. Glue baste and sew. Complete the outer garment.

Assemble the lining and hem the sleeves. Place the lining in the garment, wrong sides together, matching armscye and side seams. Turn under the front and neck edges of the lining and pin it in place on the zipper tape. Clip and adjust to fit the neckline and front edge curves. Separate the zipper and stitch it to the lining. Hem the lining. Sew a button at the hem of the garment sleeve. Make a loop at the hem of the sleeve lining.

LINED VESTS

In vests, as in other garments, lining adds to the wearing comfort and prolongs the life of the garment. Edge-to-edge lining is the most successful. Lining can be applied to the vest with wrong sides together and binding around the outer edges, or the two can be sewn with right sides together, then turned. For either technique, cut the lining from the garment pattern pieces. Because there are no sleeves to create stress on the lining, a release pleat at the center back is not needed.

Lined Vest With Bound Edges

Cut the vest and the lining, removing the seam allowances around the armscye, front and neck edges, and lower edge. Add any desired embellishment and complete the outer vest.

Construct the lining and press the seams open. Glue baste the vest to the lining, wrong sides together, at armholes and all around neck, front, and lower edges. Bind the edges with leather or suede as described on page 79.

Lining can be applied to a vest with wrong sides together and the outer edges then bound, or the two can be stitched with right sides together, then turned. A combination of the two techniques was used for this pigsuede and silk/wool vest. The separating zipper was applied with a decorative machine stitch. The unique pocket was designed to make use of an interesting edge of the skin.

A back and binding of lamb frame the handwoven chenille vest front. Thin strips of leather are twisted into ropes and worked into the overall pattern to form the button loop.

Lined Vest with Seamed Edges

Add embellishment to the outer vest pieces. Stitch the fronts to the back just at the shoulders. Join the lining sections at the shoulders and press the seams open.

With right sides together, clip the lining to vest at armscyes and all around the front, neck, and lower edges. Stitch, trim, and clip as necessary.

Turn the vest to the right side by reaching through one of the open side back seams and pulling each front through its shoulder (figure 7.12). Lightly press the lining. Pound the seams with a mallet.

To prevent the lining rolling outward when the garment is worn, glue baste the leather seam allowances in place. Topstitch if desired.

With right sides together and the raw edges even, clip the garment side seams together. To stitch, begin sewing the lining 1 inch (2.5 cm) below the hemline, continue up the side of the vest and 1 inch (2.5 cm) past the armhole onto the lining. Finger press seam allowances open. Pound with a mallet and sew or cement them in place.

Smooth out the lining. Slipstitch the remainder of each lining side seam (figure 7.13).

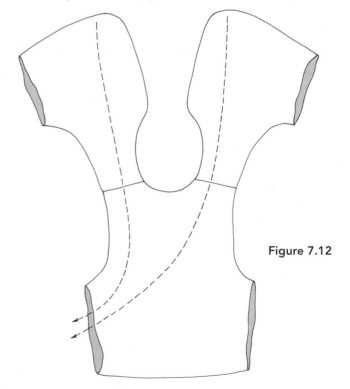

Figure 7.12

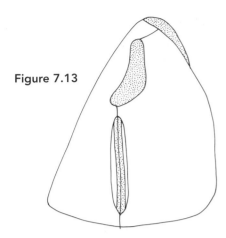

Figure 7.13

DRESS LININGS AND FACINGS

Dresses hang better and feel more comfortable when they are lined. An edge-to-edge lining is softer against the skin, and eliminates the need for facings. If facings are desired, make them of fabric that is compatible with the garment. Use interfacing of an appropriate weight. Understitch to prevent the seams from rolling outward.

Lining Blouses

Blouses of soft, thin leather or suede generally are unlined. A close-fitting shell might be lined for wearing comfort and to prevent crocking of color onto the body or undergarments.

Also in the interest of wearing comfort, a partial lining might be included. The body of a shirt can be lined, or just a portion of the body, such as the shoulder area. In sportswear it is typical to line yokes, and to face neckbands and sleeve cuffs with fabric.

The simplest pattern produces a striking garment when it is made up in rich pigsuede. Patterned silk and contrasting pigsuede provide the accents and make it the sewer's own.

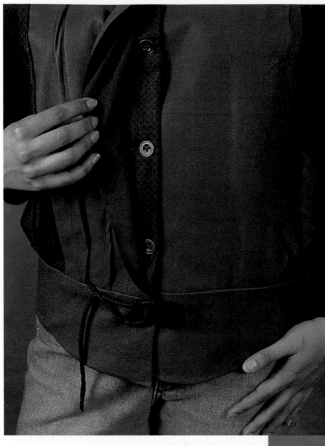

With a basic pattern, delectable materials, and a good sense of sewing fun, you can create a one-of-a-kind garment every time. This pigsuede and cotton print vest exhibits plenty of imagination in the combination of materials and techniques. The designer added random tucks and lines of stitching, with corded fabric tubing for the unusual closures. Note that the reverse side of the pigsuede was used. The hidden button placket is shown above.

CHAPTER 8

Accents and Embellishments

Hand-worked French knots secure the overlapping layers on a jacket yoke. The jacket is shown on page 96.

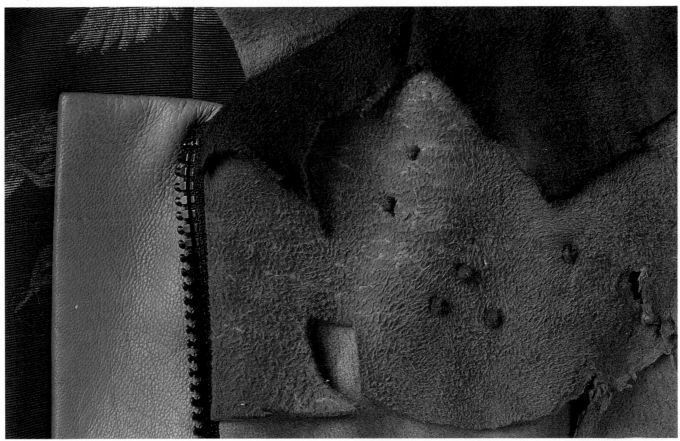

Having a broad selection of embellishment and closure techniques in your repertoire increases your design freedom. Use the ideas in this chapter as a springboard for creativity. Try experimenting with some of the modern textile techniques if they suit your design. In addition, the special qualities of leather and suede allow for the creation of effects that can't be achieved with textiles. Textures and interesting edges can be incorporated into a design scheme that is unique to your project.

Textile garments embellished with leather or suede have increased drama or sophistication. Leather or suede binding on handwoven textiles is a fitting accent. Pockets or closures of leather focus attention subtly or exuberantly. Familiarity with the material breeds confidence in working with it, so play for a while before deciding exactly which techniques will be used for the current garment or project.

When you experiment, make samples on scraps and keep notes. You will be able to duplicate the results when you wish to use the idea in a future design. On pages 124 to 125, you will find pattern information for the garments in this chapter.

OVERLAPPING LAYERS

Layering the rough, uneven edges of skins and hides into a cascading pattern can be an interesting design element. To create this effect, apply the leather layers to a fabric underlining cut from the pattern piece. For the underlining, use fabric in a weight compatible with your leather. Use polyester or poly/cotton broadcloth for lighter weight suedes and leathers. For heavier leathers, use a heavier underlining such as the poly/rayon blend made for interfacing men's neckties.

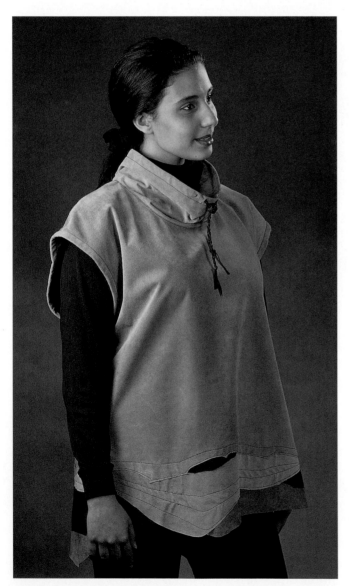

Overlapping layers of pigsuede are highlighted with machine stitching in contrasting colors. Thin strips of suede are twisted into a cord to accent the collar.

Plan the layout. Position the lowest piece first and secure it to the underlining with a glue stick. Stitch it to the underlining, stitching across the upper edge of the leather so the stitching will be hidden by subsequent layers of leather. Repeat with additional layers, working upward, until all pieces have been applied. The underlying area of a piece must be stitched for security, but the overlapping edge or area may be stitched decoratively by hand or machine or it can be permanently cemented. The jacket pictured here is a good example of this technique.

REVERSE FACINGS

Facings are normally applied and finished to the inside of a garment. Changing the procedure so the facing is applied on the inside, then turned and finished to the outside, finishes and embellishes in one step. Try utilizing the rough edges of a skin or hide in an exposed facing. If a finished edge is preferred at the outer facing edges, bind or finish as desired, then apply the facing to the garment.

Cut the facings, using the pattern piece as a guide for the edge(s) that will be sewn to the garment. The outer free edge can be any shape. Remember to add seam allowance as necessary to the desired finished width of the facing.

Apply the right side of the facing to the wrong side of the garment. Stitch, then understitch through the garment and seam allowances. Trim and grade the seam allowances. Turn the facing to the right side of the garment and topstitch along the outer facing edge.

FACED SHAPES FOR BUTTONHOLES
OR POCKET OPENINGS

Distinctive buttonholes and pockets can be made in any size or shape with this technique. When just a small amount of the facing is visible around an opening, it creates an effect similar to piping, but with less work. The opening can be any shape or size, but plan the design so the opening will be far enough away from edges and hems that it will not interfere with construction. Leather, suede, or textile can be used for the facing.

Interface the background leather or suede in the design area. Mark the shape of the opening on the wrong side of the interfaced background. Cut facing material 1 to 2 inches (2.5 to 5 cm) larger than the opening to be faced. Glue baste within the marked design area.

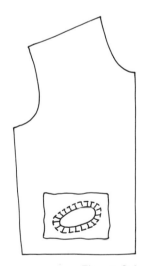

Reverse facings of lamb-skin, with a peplum to match, complement the antique kimono silk used in this very feminine vest. A close-up of the distinctive closure is shown on page 107.

Place the facing and background with right sides together and stitch around the marked line (figure 8.1). Cut away the leather and facing within the stitched design, leaving a narrow graded seam allowance. Clip or notch as necessary and turn the facing to the wrong side. Leave a small amount of the facing exposed to simulate the appearance of piping.

To make a buttonhole, form welts of suede, leather, or fabric that has been interfaced as required (detailed instructions for buttonholes are on pages 81 to 82). Glue baste in place behind the opening, then topstitch to secure (figure 8.2). Trim and grade to reduce bulk.

A pocket opening is made the same way. Topstitch, then add a backing layer. Stitch to form pocket bag.

For a less sporty look, eliminate the topstitching. Instead, fold back the garment to expose the seam allowances then stitch through the seam allowances, welts, and the backing if one was used.

Figure 8.1   **Figure 8.2**

Interwoven sewn silk tubes make a nicely textured faced shape opening. And the buttonholes happen automatically!

ALTERNATIVE CLOSURES

Loops, ties, tabs, and buckles, and their countless variations, are successful alternatives to traditional buttons and buttonholes. Use them singly or in combination to turn an ordinary garment into one that is special and individual. The personal style you express can range from simple and elegant to wildly eccentric. Incorporate favorite objects or treasures into your own closure design.

A pair of silver-toned buttons provides a simple and effective closure for the vest front. A length of cording is sewn in place around one button and loops over the other. The closure design is repeated as an accent on the pocket.

To form the distinctive button loop for this chenille vest, thin strips of leather are twisted into ropes that complement the overall pattern.

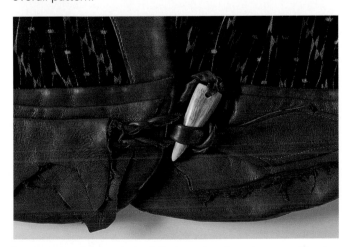

Leather inspires wonderfully imaginative closures. On the waistband of this vest, a horn toggle is attached with twisted leather strips and slips into a shaped leather loop on the opposite side. The vest is shown on page 105.

APPLIQUÉ

Whether the design is elaborate or simple, the basic appliqué technique remains the same: shapes are stitched onto a larger background piece to create interesting effects. With heavier leather, simply cut out the desired shape, position it on the background piece with glue stick or spray adhesive, and stitch. Appliqué provides a good opportunity to try decorative stitches.

Lighter weight leather and suede require more support. Apply iron-on interfacing (test it first on a scrap) to the back of the appliqué leather. Draw the desired shape on the stabilizer side, remembering to reverse the image. When applied, the right side will be exposed. Position the piece on the garment with glue stick or spray adhesive. With lightweight background leather, add a layer of tear-away stabilizer under it. Sew the design pieces in place with plain or decorative stitches.

REVERSE APPLIQUÉ

This technique is remarkably easy with leather or suede. The accent material is placed under the main piece and the design area cut away to expose the accent beneath. The accent can be leather, suede or textile as long as it is of similar weight or is interfaced to be of similar weight to the principal suede or leather. This is a terrific way to showcase specialty needlework or stenciling.

With a fine-tipped marker, draw the design shape in its correct position on the right side of the main leather piece. The line should be a generous ⅛ inch (3 mm) inside the intended stitching line. Place the accent material right side up behind the design. Sew around the design through both layers, making sure the stitching lines just meet. Do not overlap stitching. Pull the thread ends to the back of the work and tie them securely.

Using appliqué scissors, work from the right side and carefully cut away the leather within the design shape, leaving the accent material intact. Cut close to the stitching, making sure to remove all of the drawn lines.

The natural edges of a cowhide piece define the applique at the yoke of a jeans jacket. For the pocket trim, the same cowhide is used with darker pigsuede for accent.

A recycled suede skirt, complete with hip pockets, adorns the jacket back. The skirt provided plenty of scraps to work into the garment design; the leather was just too nice to be discarded.

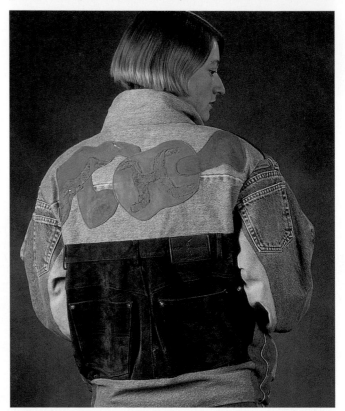

Reverse appliqué is featured on this vest, a modification of the vest described on page 50. Purchased bead fringe adds movement and a bit of glitz.

Cotton print fabric and vibrant red pigsuede make a delightful combination for reverse applique. For added sparkle, it was stitched with metallic thread.

For a simple experiment in piecing leather, try a cap! Instructions appear on page 61.

PIECING

A wonderful way to use up scraps of lightweight leather and suede is to piece them into quilt designs. Any design will work if a few guidelines are followed.

> Combine leathers of similar weight, or interface the lighter ones to the weight of the heavier pieces.
>
> Interface soft leathers to stabilize them.
>
> Overlap or abut the edges of the pieces.
>
> Join the pieces with zigzag or decorative stitches.

Piecing can be worked directly onto a fabric backing. Cut the backing from the pattern with generous seam allowances. Complete the piecing and any quilting, then trim to the pattern.

QUILTING

Many designs are enhanced by the warmth and dimensional look that quilting can add. There are a variety of materials that can be used as batting in garments, each producing different results. Thinner material gives subtle dimension to a free-form design. Heavier batting insulates better and gives deeper dimension. Lighter weight leathers are best for quilting. The loft is lost if heavier leather is used, and the resulting garment is unyielding and stiff to wear.

As a rule, quilt first, then cut pieces to the pattern. If garment pieces are cut before quilting is done, allow generous seam allowances, as quilting tends to shrink an area.

When a thin batting is used, such as flannel, cut the garment and batting pieces by the pattern, but with additional seam allowance. Use spray adhesive to bond them together temporarily. Draw the quilting lines on the batting with a fine-tipped marker and use these lines as a guide for stitching. Begin at the center of the design and work outward, alternating stitching direction with each row of stitching (figure 8.3 on page 111).

To avoid damage by the feed dogs on smooth leathers, use a Hera marker on the leather surface to make guide lines. Sew with the right side up.

Figure 8.3

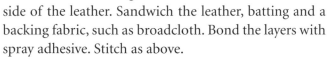

For a fuller look, use unbonded polyester batting, up to a six-ounce weight, or try polyurethane foam. Mark quilting lines with chalk or a Hera marker on the right side of the leather. Sandwich the leather, batting and a backing fabric, such as broadcloth. Bond the layers with spray adhesive. Stitch as above.

Bonded batting may be quilted to leather without a backing fabric. Place bonded side of batting down and lay the leather right side up on top. Bond with spray adhesive. Stitch as above.

MACHINE EMBROIDERY

Many of today's home sewing machines are equipped with the ability to do extraordinary embroidery patterns. Most require the use of a hoop, which in turn is attached to the embroidery unit. Securing leather or suede in a hoop can stretch or damage it. Heavier leather won't fit into a hoop. Instead, use an adhesive-backed stabilizer to secure the leather for stitching. New stabilizers are being developed constantly to ease and simplify the procedure. Always test the stabilizer on a scrap.

Most of the new machine embroidery threads can be used successfully on leather. Specialty needles, such as those developed for use with metallic threads or for free-motion stitching, may be helpful.

Work stitching samples before beginning embroidery on the project itself. Subtle changes in tension make a big difference in the finished product.

Free-motion embroidery also can be very effective. Use an adhesive-backed stabilizer, and experiment with scraps before beginning a project.

A vest of soft plongé features a free-form machine-quilted design. To keep the surface free of wrinkles, alternate stitching direction of the quilting lines.

Machine embroidery on lightweight leather and suede was worked with decorative rayon and metallic threads.

WEAVING

Spectacular effects can be created when woven patterns are incorporated into a design or used for an entire garment. Since leather and suede don't ravel, it is not necessary to finish the edges of strips used for weaving. Whether the design is simple or intricate, the basic concept remains the same: strips are interlaced at angles to one another to create a new material. Secure the resulting "fabric" to a backing and integrate it into the garment. Cement or stitch the strip ends to secure them. (Figure 8.4.)

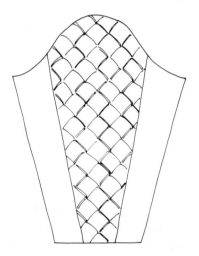

Figure 8.4. Interwoven strips of leather or suede can be used for an entire garment section or a decorative inset.

A stylized fish motif, stenciled along the front and on the rear pocket, adds a note of sophisticated whimsy to this pigsuede tunic.

STENCILING AND STAMPING

Sueded, rough textures are best for stenciling and stamping. The paint is better able to adhere, and the results are most impressive.

Read the manufacturer's directions before purchasing paints for use on leather. Some brands require the addition of bonding agents or catalysts. Some may call for heat setting with a hot iron, which is not an option for leather. Instead, use a hair dryer set on high heat for a few minutes.

The key to successful stenciling is to use a very slightly damp sponge and a very small amount of paint. If more color is needed, simply layer it until the desired effect is achieved.

FRINGE

A decorative fringe can be made by simply cutting parallel lines cut in a strip of leather. To make a strip of fringe, calculate the length and width required and add seam allowances as necessary. Use a clear ruler and rotary cutter for even cuts, working from the edge to the seam allowance (photo 1).

Photo 1. Twisted fringe is made by wetting the leather after cutting, then twisting it. Pin it to hold it in place until it dries. This technique works well with soft, thin leather.

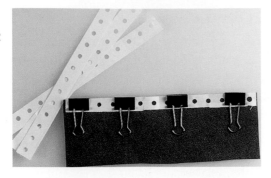

Photo 2

Photo 3

Photo 4

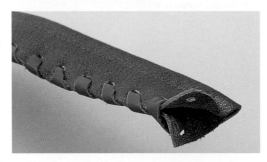

Photo 5

Photo 6

Photo 7

LACING

As embellishment or as a closure, lacing adapts well to leather garments and projects. Purchased lacing is available in a limited color range. To lace edges together with a whipstitch as shown in the examples requires lacing approximately three and one-half times the length of the edge.

The following technique makes quick work of lacing together two leather pieces. To make holes that are well spaced and uniform, use the perforated strip from computer paper as a template. Clip it to the edge to be laced. Use punch pliers to make the holes, cutting the smallest hole that will accommodate the lacing (photo 2).

To make lacing, begin with a circular piece of leather. Starting at the edge, cut toward the center in a spiral to produce a single strip even in width. A circle 6 inches (15 cm) in diameter yields a considerable length of narrow lacing.

Special lacing needles are available but are not always needed. Cut the lacing end to a tapered point and pull it through the lacing holes by hand. Secure the lace at the beginning and end with permanent contact cement (photos 3 through 6), or catch it in the seam if the pieces will be stitched. Lacing can be functional or serve as a decorative element (photo 7).

KNIT CUFFS, COLLARS AND HEMS

Leather garments often are designed with knit finishes for sleeves, necklines, and lower edges. Knit fabric is comfortable against the skin and its flexibility allows ease of movement.

Select knit fabric of a weight compatible to that of the garment leather. As an alternative to knit yardage, try a pair of socks! Socks are inexpensive and come in a vast array of styles, colors, and weights. The ankle portion can be used for cuffs, or sewn together to make a collar.

For a sleeve, snip off the sock ribbing at the ankle. Fold it in half and apply to the sleeve end, adjusting the total sleeve length as necessary to accommodate the "cuff." To make a collar, cut off the ankle portions of two or several matching socks, slash them open, and join the ends to create enough length for the pattern piece. Cut and sew according to pattern instructions.

If it is necessary to gather a considerable length of leather onto a knit sleeve or hem, gather all or part of the leather edge with a machine basting stitch. This will prevent having to overstretch the knit.

BEADING

There are entire books devoted to the art of beading. Owing to the recent popularity of the art, there is a magnificent array of beads from which to choose. Embellishment with a small amount of beading can change a wonderful garment into a stunning garment.

In selecting beads, choose those without sharp edges that might cut either the leather or the thread. Make sure the holes in the beads will accommodate a threaded needle.

Regular beading needles may be too flimsy to penetrate the leather. Instead, use a shorter, stronger needle, such as a 12 sharp. Experiment to find one that will penetrate the leather without bending. With very lightweight leather, use woven fabric as a backing to support the beadwork. Choose material with a compatible hand to that of the leather.

A variety of threads may be used. Try samples before beginning a project to see what gives the best results. Remember to avoid 100 percent cotton thread. Avoid nylon and rayon threads too; nylon can cut the leather and rayon embroidery thread will not withstand the abrasion of normal wear. Long-staple polyester or cotton-wrapped polyester threads are best. Fine dental floss and linen threads also can be used.

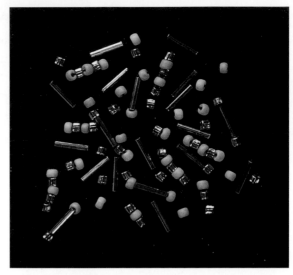

A delicate beaded design is worked on lightweight pigsuede.

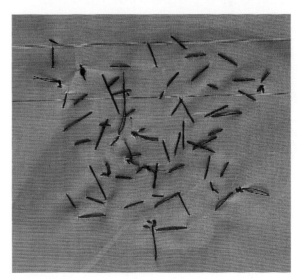

Sheer polyester organza provides a thin but firm backing to support the beading.

CHAPTER 9

Care and Cleaning of Leather and Suede

With proper care, leather and suede garments will last a long, long time. Their care requirements differ from those of fabric garments, but they generally require far less attention and are far more durable.

Storage of Hides and Skins

Until you are ready to cut into them, keep skins rolled on cardboard tubes such as those from home decorator fabrics. Wrap the rolls in plain brown kraft paper. Several skins or hides can be stored on a single roll. Do not fold the skins; foldlines become permanent marks that cannot be removed. Do not be tempted to wrap the rolled and paper-wrapped leather in an outer layer of plastic. Leather needs to breathe and plastic prevents this.

Store skins away from heat, light, and moisture. Heat will dry the leather, causing it to become stiff and unsupple. Light will fade colors, especially blue, green, purple, and brown. Moisture promotes bacterial and fungal growth that permanently damages the skin or hide.

Washing Leather and Suede

Originally, tanned skins and hides were not designed to be washed. That isn't necessarily the case today. Advances in technology have given us washable leather and suede. The supplier will include specific washing instructions when you buy a washable skin. A mild soap such as shampoo is often suggested.

Leather and suede, even that designated as washable, will shrink when it is washed, often substantially. Prewash the skin to reduce shrinkage of the garment. Make sure all the other construction materials, such as lining and interfacing, have similar washing requirements, and preshrink them by washing them as you do the leather.

Repeated washing can reduce the supple hand of the leather. Treat the garment occasionally with products designed to restore the original finish.

Lambsuede and pigsuede that are not designated as washable sometimes can be washed with reasonable success. For shirts and other garments worn close to the body, this is desirable. Both kinds of suede will shrink quite a bit, and the color and hand will be altered.

Wash the skins with mild soap and tepid water. Dry in the dryer at a low heat setting. A towel tossed in along with the skins will help soften them. Preshrink the skins and other construction materials by washing them before cutting out the garment.

Remember that washing is not the preferred method of cleaning leather and suede, but an alternative. As such, it requires experimentation.

Washable lining and interfacing were used in these washable leather pants. The zipper is rustproof; the button is plastic. See pattern information, page 124.

Garment Care and Maintenance

Leather has a long life span. The material is strong and durable, offering a lifetime of enjoyment. With proper care, a leather garment can last indefinitely and actually improve with wear, conforming to the body and becoming more comfortable.

These samples of pigsuede and lambsuede indicate the amount of shrinkage that resulted from laundering. Note that color and texture were lost as well. These skins were tanned in the conventional way; they were not treated to make them washable.

PROTECTING YOUR LEATHER GARMENTS

Take precautions during the construction process to prevent stains on the leather. Cements can bleed through the leather and cause discoloration on the right side. Glue baste only in the seam allowances, and apply cement moderately.

If highly contrasting leather colors are combined in a garment, the colors may bleed when the garment is cleaned. The same is true of contrasting leather/textile combinations.

Guard against stains by spraying a new or recently cleaned suede or leather with a topical spray designed to repel water, stains and soil. Products meant for use on smooth leather differ from those intended for suede; be sure to use the correct type. Test any such product on an inconspicuous part of the garment, such as the underside of the hem. Do not use water and stain repellents on soiled garments.

Stain repellents should be reapplied after the garment is dry cleaned or washed. Dry cleaners can apply them when you have a garment cleaned.

Like skins, garments should be stored away from heat, light, and moisture. Use padded hangers for coats and tops. For skirts or pants, add hanger loops during construction, or use a small piece of the same leather between hanger clips and the garment to prevent marks. Use fabric, not plastic, bags to protect garments from dust. Pillowcases are usually just the right size for jackets.

Most wrinkles will hang out. If pressing is necessary, iron at moderate temperature setting with no steam. Use plain brown kraft paper as a press "cloth." Don't press a damp garment.

Perfume, hair spray, pins, adhesive badges and tape can damage leather. Wear dress shields and scarves to protect leather worn close to the body.

Should you be caught in the rain in your leather jacket, blot away excess water with a towel, then air dry the garment away from heat. For suede, restore the nap with a suede brush when the garment is dry. Allow the garment to dry thoroughly before pressing.

HOME CARE FOR LEATHER AND SUEDE

Clean smooth leather with a damp, soft cloth; wire brushes or other abrasives can damage the surface. Dry with a soft cloth. Oil spots can be removed or reduced with cornmeal. Sprinkle it on and rub it in, then let it set several hours or longer. Brush off the residue with a soft cloth. Repeat the process if necessary. Fuller's earth or talcum powder may be used instead of cornmeal.

A gum eraser will remove a variety of marks from leather. Glue can be removed with a ball of rubber cement. Ballpoint pen marks are difficult to remove; professional cleaning may be required.

To clean suede, use a suede brush with stiff natural or plastic bristles. A suede stone works, too. Remove oil as for smooth leather.

Leather and suede cleaning and reconditioning products intended for footwear can be used on garments. Follow the manufacturer's instructions. Do not use textile cleaning fluids for leather. Do not use saddle soap or mink oil on garment leather. Today's tanning technology is different, and these products can damage skins and hides.

Reconditioning products can be used to restore softness to a leather garment that has been cleaned several times, or simply worn for a long time and stored in a dry place. These, too, should be used only on a clean, dry garment.

PROFESSIONAL CLEANING

When dry cleaning is necessary, use a reputable cleaner with the capability of cleaning by the special process needed for leather and suede. Do not use a self-service cleaning facility for leathers. Clean all pieces of an ensemble at the same time to avoid variations in color and texture.

Be aware that cleaning can make flaws or variations in the leather more apparent, and can weaken the cement bonds. Cleaning may also eradicate surface textures, embossing, and metallic finishes.

Washable leather or old leather may need to be reconditioned occasionally. Use a product designed for the purpose, or have the garment reconditioned professionally. High quality leather and suede will have a longer life span and will require less care than will inferior grades.

Glossary

Terms and Descriptions

This section contains an alphabetical listing of common leather and suede terms, along with descriptive information about the different skins and hides.

Alligator—A general term used for leather made from the skin of any aquatic species having a grain similar to that of the American alligator.

Alligator-grained leather—This term is used to distinguish the alligator-grained effect embossed on various types of leather from genuine reptilian leather.

Aniline dyeing—A process for coloring leather with transparent dyes that allows the natural characteristics of the leather to show through, similar to the use of stain on wood. Aniline-dyed leather is usually topped with a protective coating.

Antelope—A fine, soft leather made from antelope skin, velvety in texture and sheen, sueded on the flesh side.

Back—The section that results when a hide is cut longitudinally along the backbone with the head and belly trimmed off, leaving a "bend" and shoulder.

Bark tanning—A process that utilizes vegetable materials derived from certain plants and woods, often called "bark tannins."

Bating—The removal of residual unhairing chemicals and non-leather making substances.

Belly hide—From the underside of the animal.

Bend—The portion of a hide remaining after the head, shoulder, and belly sections have been removed.

Blue—The term "in the blue" refers to hides or skins that have been chrome tanned but not finished.

Boarded leather—Leather with a grain effect produced by folding the skin grain against grain, then mechanically rolling the two surfaces against each other.

Bovine—A cow, ox, or closely related animal.

Buckskin—A term generally applied to leather from deer. Strictly speaking, only the outer cut of the skin from which the surface grain has been removed can be labeled "genuine buckskin." Leather finished from the split or undercut of deerskin must be described as "split buckskin." For garments, it is available in a 2½ ounce weight. Hides average 7 to 12 square feet (.65 to 1.12 sq m).

Buffed cowhide—*See* **Nubuck**.

Cabretta—A hair-type sheepskin from Brazil. It is soft and fine grained. Skins average 7 to 10 square feet (.65 to .93 sq m). The term is often used to refer to any smoothly finished sheepskin.

Calfskin leather—made from the skin of young cattle; available in 2½ to 3½ ounce weights. Skins average 7 to 12 square feet (.65 to 1.12 sq m).

Calf suede—Suede made from the underneath, or flesher, side of the hides of young cattle. It comes in 1 to 1½ ounce weights. Skins average 5 to 7 square feet (.47 to .65 sq m).

Capeskin or cape leather—Terms used for glove and garment leather made from sheepskin, with the natural grain preserved. The term should be confined to the leather from South African hair sheep. It is thin and fine grained and is generally superior to leather made from wool sheepskins.

Carpincho leather—Made from the hide of a water rodent indigenous to Argentina and Uruguay. It is more elastic and softer then peccary. It is generally chrome tanned and washable. It is classed as a pigskin.

Chamois—Originally made from the skins of Alpine antelope, or chamois, it is now the oil-tanned, suede-finished fleshers, or under-splits, of sheepskins. Garment chamois is sometimes lamb suede. It is available in 1¾ to 2 ounce weights. Hides average 5 to 6 square feet (.47 to .56 sq m).

Chrome retan—Leather that has been first chrome tanned then retanned with vegetable or synthetic extracts.

Chrome tanned—Tanning of leather with chromium compounds, sometimes with small amounts of some other tanning agent.

Combination tanned—Tannage with two or more agents, such as chrome and vegetable.

Corrected grain—*See* **Snuffed finish**.

Cowhide—Specifically, leather made from the hides of cows. The term is generally used to designate leather tanned from hides of animals of the bovine species. It is available in 2 to 10 ounce weights, or greater. Full hides average 50 to 60 square feet (4.65 to 5.57 sq m). Sides average 25 to 30 square feet (2.32 to 2.79 sq m).

Cowhide splits—Sueded leathers made from horizontally sectioned layers of cowhide. Usually, both sides are sueded. Garment splits are available in 2½ to 3 ounce weights. Chap hides are 4 to 4½ ounces. Hides average 6 to 9 square feet.

Crocking—Rubbing off of color or other surface substances.

Crop   A side of leather with the belly trimmed off but with the head and shoulders retained.

Crushed leather—Leather in which the natural grain is accentuated during manufacture by plating, boarding, or another process. The term also applies to leather that has been "grained" artificially.

Deep buff—The first cut under the top grain or machine buff. No traces of grain remain.

Deerskin—Leather tanned from the skin of a deer, with the grain surface intact. It is available in 2½ to 3 ounce weights. Skins average 7 to 10 square feet (.65 to .93 sq m).

Deerskin splits—Suede made from horizontally sectioned layers of deerskin. The surface is sueded on both sides.

Degrained leather—Genuine suede, finished, on the flesh side of skins from which the grain has been removed after tanning, by splitting, abrading, or another process.

Distressed leather—Leather finished by a tanning process that produces uneven coloration and markings to give a fashionable weathered look.

Doeskin—Lightweight leather from a female deer.

Elk—Soft leather similar to deerskin. It has a coarser grain and is usually too heavy to sew on a household machine. It is available in 3 to 4 ounce weights.

Embossed—Hides or skins finished with designs stamped onto them by etched, engraved, or electroplated plates or rollers.

Fancy leather—A general term to describe leather made from many kinds of hides and skins that have commercial importance and value primarily because of grain or distinctive finish, whether natural or the result of processing.

Fatliquoring—The tanning step in which oil and fatty substances are added. One of the last wet operations, this step regulates the pliability and tensile strength of the leather.

Finish—An inclusive term referring to treatments that affect the appearance and hand of the leather, and which are applied after the initial dying and tanning.

Flesher—The underneath split layer of a sheepskin used to make chamois.

Fleshing—The process of removing excess flesh and fatty substances from a hide before tanning.

Frizing—A process for removing the grain by liming. It is used in making Mocha glove leather.

Full grain—The outer cut taken from the hair side of the hide from which nothing but the hair and associated epidermis have been removed. The appearance of the grain is unchanged.

Garment leather—Any lightweight leather used to produce clothing. The term "napa leather" is sometimes used to refer to garment leather.

Garment suede—Usually refers to lamb suede; sometimes cow or pig. It is available in ¾ to 2½ ounce weights. Skin size varies with the animal.

Glazed finish—Similar to an aniline finish, but the leather is polished by the action of rollers under high pressure.

Glove leather—Sheep, pig, deer, and kid that has been tanned to produce soft stretchy leather for dress gloves. Work and garden gloves are made from cowhide splits, sheep, horse, pig, and goat.

Goatskin—The skin or leather from a mature goat, sometimes called "kid." It is available in 1½ to 2 ounce weights. Skins average 5 to 8 square feet (.47 to .74 sq m).

Grain—The outer or hair side of a skin or hide. "Grain" also refers to the pattern of the outer surface after the hair or wool and epidermal tissue have been removed.

Grain leather—*See* **Full grain**.

Hair-on leather—Leather tanned with the hair left intact.

Hairsheep—The skin from Brazilian sheep that have hair rather than wool. It is used to make cabretta leather.

Hide—The whole pelt from one of the larger animals.

In the pickle—The term describes skins from which the hair or wool has been removed, and which have been preserved with brine, acid, or polymer phosphates, and are ready for tanning. The skins usually are in a wet state.

Kangaroo—Leather made from the Australian kangaroo or wallaby. It resembles glazed kid, but has a finer grain. It is one of the strongest leathers and is usually used for footwear. It is available in 2½ ounce weights. Skins average 5 to 6 square feet.

Kid—Leather made from the skin of a young goat. In the industry, "kid" refers to any leather made from goat.

Kip or kipskin—Skin from a bovine of intermediate size.

Lambskin—Leather made from lamb or sheep, as the skins are identical in appearance after tanning. European (Spanish, Italian, or French) lambskin is considered the best; it is smooth, lightweight, and uniform, with a tight grain. English domestic is second in order of preference, followed by New Zealand. It is available in 1 to 2 ounce weights. Skins average 5 to 8 square feet (.47 to .74 sq m).

Lambskin suede—Often referred to as "garment suede," this is lambskin that has been sueded. It comes in ¾ to 2 ounce weights. Skins average 5 to 8 square feet (.47 to .74 sq m).

Leather—A general term for hide or skin with its original fibrous structure more or less intact, tanned or treated to be imputrescible. The hair or wool may or may not have been removed. Leather is also made from a hide or skin, which has been split into layers or segmented before or after tanning.

Machine buff—The cut of the hide from which a portion of the grain has been removed. Some of the grain remains, as in nubuck.

Mineral tanned—Leather produced by the use of chromium salts, aluminum, or zirconium salts.

Mocha leather—A leather made from any variety of hair sheep. After the grain has been removed by frizing, the fine fibers below the grain are sueded. It is one of the finest nap-finished glove leathers.

Naked leather—Leather with little or no finish applied to the surface. Only high-quality skins are made into naked leather. Water will stain it.

Napa—Commonly used as a synonym for "grain leather," or any smooth garment leather. Technically the term refers to sheepskin tanned in such a way that the underside of the hide has the appearance of grain leather rather than suede.

Nubuck—Leather created by lightly buffing the top grain until it takes on a very fine nap with an appearance smoother than that of suede.

Oil tanned—The process of tanning with animal oils is used in the manufacture of certain soft leathers, particularly chamois, and some kinds of buckskin. Fish oil is generally used.

Ostrich—Leather made from ostrich skin. It has characteristic markings that result from removal of the feathers from the skin.

Pasting—A method of drying leather by sticking it onto large plates which are then passed through a drying oven.

Patent leather—Leather with a finish that is mirror-like, flexible, and waterproof.

Peccary—A species of wild boar native to Central and South America, and the durable leather made from it.

Pelt—An untanned hide or skin with the hair in place.

Pigment dyed—A leather finish in which the surface is coated with pigments or other opaque materials, masking the surface somewhat or entirely. This finish is usually applied to less expensive skins to cover imperfections.

Pickling—The process of adding salt and acid to hides, which transforms them into an acid state.

Pigskin—Skin from pigs and hogs, usually made into suede. It has a grainy texture and characteristic pattern of markings where the bristles have been removed. It is available in 1 to 2 ounce weights. Skins average 10 to 14 square feet (.93 to 1.3 sq m).

Pigsuede—Synonymous with pigskin.

Plongé—Thin, fine cowhide originally from Japanese cows fed a beer diet. Good quality plongé is now produced in other countries, as well. Large hide size and more moderate price make it a good choice for garments. It is available in 1½ to 2 ounce weights. Hides average 50 to 60 square feet (4.65 to 5.57 sq m); sides average 18 to 25 square feet (1.7 to 2.32 sq m).

Rawhide—Cattle hide that has been dehaired and limed, often stuffed or greased, but that has not been tanned.

Retanned leather—Leather that has been tanned a second time with similar or different tanning materials.

Semi-analine leather—Leather finished with a combination of analine dyes and pigments. This process evens out the shading.

Shearling—Sheepskin finished with the wool left on. In garments, the wool may be inside or outside. The non-wool side may have a suede or a smooth finish. Weight is determined by pile depth: shearling with ¾-inch (2 cm) pile is approximately a 1½ ounce weight.

Side—Half of a whole hide that has been cut longitudinally.

Skin—Pelt from a young or small animal.

Skiver—Thin splits of calf, pig or sheep.

Snuffed finish—Grain leather with the hair removed, lightly buffed. Also known as "corrected grain."

Spew—This is a result of a defect in the tanning process. It is characterized by a white coating or dark crystals of natural oil on the surface of the leather.

Split—The under portion of a hide or skin that has been divided into two or more thicknesses. The top, or grain, layer has been removed. A split may be sueded on both sides, or it can be pigment finished and embossed.

Splitting and shaving—Adjusting the thickness to that required for the end use.

Staking—Mechanical softening of leather.

Stuffed—This is a finish usually applied to heavier leather. Wax or grease is worked into the substance of the leather for the purpose of water-proofing and protection from ultra-violet light. Leather processed this way is used for footwear and saddlery.

Suede—A finish produced by abrading the surface of leather to give it a nap. The grain side of leather may be suede finished, but the process is most often applied to the flesh surface. The term denotes a finish, not a type of leather.

Toggling—A method of drying leather that is held in a stretched position with clips, or "toggles."

Top grain—The top outer layer of a hide from which nothing has been removed except the hair and associated epidermis.

Unhairing—A process of removing the hair, prior to tanning, with a solution of calcium hydroxide and sodium sulfite.

Vegetable tanned—Leather that has been tanned using vegetable products containing tannins.

Velvet finish—Suede finish.

Washable leather—Leather that can be can be laundered by standard methods and still retain its dimension, color and other physical characteristics.

Water-repellent leather—Leather that has been treated with any of several chemical compounds to repel the absorption of external water.

Leather Thickness Conversion

In the U.S., leather thickness is expressed as the weight in ounces per square foot of skin. In Europe, actual thickness in millimeters is used instead.

WEIGHT IN OUNCES PER PER SQ. FT.	THICKNESS IN INCHES	THICKNESS IN MM
1	¹⁄₆₄	0.4
2	¹⁄₃₂	0.8
3	³⁄₆₄	1.2
4	¹⁄₁₆	1.6

Patterns & Credits

Chapter 1

page 8 (also shown on page 45)

Lavender pigsuede tie belt with skirt and vest

a. Skirt pattern, Design & Sew #319

b. Vest, pinwoven with hemp; pattern available through Lois Ericson, see Sources for address

page 14 (also shown on page 98)

Whisky suit, whisky and pine distressed lamb and ostrich

a. Jacket, lined in polyester satin; pattern, Design & Sew #312; available through author, see Sources for address

b. Wrap skirt, self-draft pattern

c. Blouse, self-draft pattern

Chapter 2

page 17

Black cowhide backpack

Pattern, Shapes in Leather and Suede #311; available through author, see Sources for address

page 22

a. Milano vest, fawn pigsuede and gray/taupe wool.

Pattern, Shapes in Leather & Suede #310; available through author, see Sources for address

b. Wrap skirt, McCall's #7546

page 23

Metropolitan Spice Jacket

a. Sunflower/forest suede

b. Rose floral, caramel leather triangles on back

Pattern, Sew What's New #401, see Sources for address

page 24

a. Seven-eights length coat, teal plongé/grape suede/cotton tapestry; self-draft pattern

b. Olive pigsuede jeans; owner, Marcy Tilton

Chapter 5

page 44

a. Brown distressed cowhide belt with cap rivets and metal eyelets and silver metal buckle (also shown on page 46)

b. Seafoam pigsuede vest, stenciled, with glued beads; self-draft pattern; stencil by Revisions, see Sources for address

c. Cognac glued lamb purse lined with chocolate deersuede; owner of original bag, Carol Parks; redesigned by author, patterns on pages 54-55

d. Cognac/saddle pigsuede cap, patterns on page 61

page 48

Black cabretta belt with silver conchos, designed by author

page 50

Saddle/raisin reversible vest; side one, stenciled; side two, charms; stencil by Revisions, see Sources for address

Self-draft pattern

page 51

Saddle/lavender pigsuede vest

Self-draft pattern; stencil, author's design

page 52

a. Navy pigsuede with silk ribbons and buttons; self-draft pattern

b. Peach ostrich with lavender pigsuede, stenciled; self-draft pattern

c. Forest/red/black pigsuede with bead fringe, reverse applique; self-draft pattern (also shown on page 108)

page 59

Black cowhide purse with zebra stenciled hair-on calf

Designed by author

Chapter 6

page 63

Navy plongé vest with silver and pewter buttons

Pattern, Design & Sew #312, available through author

page 72

Mint pigsuede big shirt

Pattern, Burda World of Fashion #134; snaps: Vario snaps, see Sources for address

page 75

Black pigsuede Miyake wrap skirt

Pattern, Vogue #1693

page 78

Teal plongé/black pigsuede vest, with silk brocade facings and buttons

Pattern, Design & Sew 312, available through author

page 80

"Tea Time" long vest

Pattern, Design & Sew #312, available through author

page 81 (also shown on page 117)

Espresso washable cow pants

Pattern, Burda #3586

page 83

a. Navy mohair boucle jacket with turquoise cowhide binding;

Pattern, New Mode #21755

b. Turquoise mock wrap skirt

Pattern, New Look #6902

Chapter 7

page 86

Distressed lamb tunic in navy, chocolate, and saddle, with self-lining and designer buttons

Pattern, Design & Sew #318

page 88

a. Black pigsuede/olive square vest with taupe silk/wool blend

Pattern, Design & Sew #313, available through Lois Ericson or Diane Ericson, see Sources for address

b. Origami skirt, The Sewing Workshop, see Sources for address

page 89

Teal pigsuede skirt with silver/turquoise buttons

Designer/owner, Marcy Tilton; buttons, Paco Despacio, see Sources for address

page 92

Jeans and forest pigsuede jacket with glass buttons and green and black lining

Pattern, Paw Prints #003, through Purrfection; see Sources for address

page 96

Black cow and various shades of pigsuede and mauve lamb jacket

Designed by author

page 99

Navy/antelope pigsuede square vest with navy/taupe silk and navy/black wool

Pattern, Design & Sew #313, available through Lois Ericson or Diane Ericson; see Sources for address

page 100

Handwoven chenille vest with mauve lamp back and binding

Self-draft pattern

page 101

Raisin/navy pigsuede with gold/raisin/navy silk

Pattern, Burda #3934

page 102

Burgundy pigsuede vest with black and burgundy cotton

Pattern, Design and Sew #312, available through author

Chapter 8

page 104

Antelope/salmon/raisin pigsuede tunic with Bemberg rayon lining

Pattern, Burda #3934

page 105

Eggplant and mauve antique kimono fabric vest with mauve lamb

Pattern, Design & Sew #312, available through author

page 106

Navy/turquoise cowhide vest with silk facings and closure

Pattern, Design & Sew #312, available through author

page 108

Jeans jacket with chocolate suede and caramel leather, with sunflower print cotton lining

Pattern: Paw Prints #003 from Purrfection, see Sources for address

page 109

Jeans jacket with red pigsuede and American flag lining and star embellishment

Pattern, Paw Prints #003 from Purrfection, see Sources for address

page 110

Navy/raisin pigsuede cap, bill interfaced with buckram, self-covered buttons, designer, Nancy Cornelius

page 113

Cobalt/citron pigsuede tunic with stencils

Pattern, Burda #3934; stencils by author

Sources

Wholesale and Retail Suppliers

Leather

UNITED STATES

CINEMA LEATHERS, INC.
9555 Owensmouth Avenue #1
Chatsworth, CA 91311-4811
818-772-4600

D'ANTON LEATHERS
5530 Vincent Avenue N.E.
West Branch, IA 52358
319-643-2568

LIBRA LEATHER, INC.
259 West 30th Street
New York, NY 10001
212/695-3114
fax: 212/629-5346

R. L. COX FUR AND HIDE COMPANY
P.O. Box 25321
708 First Street N.W.
Albuquerque, NM 87125
505-242-4980

TANDY LEATHER COMPANY
8117 Hwy. 80 W.
Fort Worth, TX 76116
817-244-6404
This is the corporate address. There are many retail locations throughout the U.S.

THE HIDE AND LEATHER HOUSE
595 Monroe Street
707-255-6160
P.O. Box 509
Napa, CA 94559
Orders 800/4LEATHER
Fax 707/226-8527

CANADA

DOMINION TANNERS
1601 Church Avenue
Winnipeg, Manitoba, Canada
R2X1G9
1-204-633-7042

UNITED KINGDOM

A & A CRACK
18 Henry Street
Northampton, Northhamptonshire
UK NN1 4JE
tel: 44 1604 232135

MIDGLEY A.W. & SON LTD.
Combe Batch, Wedmore
Somerset
B S28 4DU
tel: 44 01934 712837

GERMANY

FERDINAND DETMER
Stresemann St. 108B
Hamburg
011 49 4043 8040

Patterns & Stencils

LOIS ERICSON
P.O. Box 5222
Salem, OR 97304

PURRFECTION: ARTISTIC WEARABLES
19618 Canyon Drive
Granite Falls, WA 98252

REVISIONS
Diane Ericson
P.O. Box 7404
Carmel, CA 93921

SANDY SCRIVANO
5400 Alder Glen Court
Carmichael, CA 95608

SEW WHAT'S NEW
377 W. 2nd Street, Box 7000
Sumas, WA 98295 or
34825 High Drive
Abbotsford, BC, V25 2X7

THE SEWING WORKSHOP
2010 Balboa Street
San Francisco, CA 94121

Buttons & Snaps

PACO DESPACIO
P.O. Box 2161
Cave Junction, OR 97523
541-592-4196

VARIO SNAPS
(distributed in the U.S. through)
Birch Street Clothing
P.O. Box 6901
San Mateo, CA 94403

Teflon Feet & Teflon Sheets

THE SEWING EMPORIUM
1079 Third Avenue #B
Chula Vista, CA 91910
619-420-3490

Note: Barge cement is available at leather dealers and shoe repair stores. Hera markers are available through notions suppliers.

Index

Appliqué, 106

Backstitching, hand, 23

Basting, 32; with binder clips, 32; with glue stick, 32

Bating, 10

Beading, 115; needles for, 115; selection of beads for, 115; threads for, 115

Belts, 45–47; concha belts, 48

Binding, 79–80

Blouse linings, 101

Buffing, 13

Buttons, 84; barrel, 84; Chinese knot, 84; reinforcing of, 84; self-covered, 84; toggle, 84

Buttonholes, 81–82; bound, 82; facings for, 104–105; in-seam, 82; machine, 82; with inter-facings, 64

Cap rivets, 47

Caps, 60–62; visors for, 61

Chalk wheels, 31

Closures, 106

Coat linings, 97–98

Collars, 72–74; knit, 114; pointed, 74; turning points of, 72

Conditioning, 12

Construction details, marking of, 94

Cording, 79; covered, 79

Corners, sharp, finishing of, 34

Crocking, 20

Cuffs, 72; knit, 114

Cut edges, finishing, 35

Cutting tools: appliqué scissors, 28; mats, 28; rotary cutters, 28; tailors' points, 28; trimming scissors, 28

Darts, 66–68; lapped, 68; slot, 68

Dress linings, 101

Dry milling, 12

Dyeing, pigment, 12

Dyes, aniline, 12

Embossing, 13

Embroidery, machine, 111; free-motion, 111

Exotic leathers, characteristics of, 18

Facings: dress, 101; for buttonholes, 104–105; for pockets, 104–105; reverse, 104

Fatliquoring, 12

Feed dogs, 33

Finishing tips, 35

Fringes, 113

Garments: leathers for, 17–18; protection of, 118

Grading, 14

Grainlines, 90–91

Hand-sewing tools: awls, 30; beading needles, 27, 30; glovers' needles, 27, 30

Hats, 60–62; visors for, 61

Hems, 69; knit, 114

Hera marker, 31

Hides: defined, 15; size chart, 21; size of, 21; storage of, 117

Interfacings, 64, 65; selection of, 64; testing of, 65; where to use, 64; with buttonholes, 64

Jacket linings, 97–98

Kip, defined, 15

Lacing, 114

Lambsuede, washing of, 117

Layers, overlapping, 104; planning layout for, 104

Leather: from cattle, 18; from deer family, 18; from goats and kids, 18; from pigs and hogs, 18; from sheep and lambs, 18; defects in, 19; defined, 15; grades of, 19; professional cleaning of, 119; reconditioning of, 119; removal of oil spots from, 119; selection of, 19–22; categories of, 18; structure of, 8; thickness of, 19; washing of, 116; weights of, 20

Leather-cutting checklist, 94

Leathers, fancy, characteristics of, 18

Leftover pieces, uses for, 22

Linings, 90, 95; bagged, 97–98; choice of fabric for, 95; for blouses, 101; for coats, 97–98; for dresses, 101; for jackets, 97–98; for pants, 95; for skirts, 95–97; for vests, 99-100; hems for, 95–97; removable, 98; zip-in, 98

Measuring, 14

Napped skins, 91

Notions, 31

Pants linings, 95

Pattern weights, 94

Patterned skins, 91

Patterns: choosing of, 87; cutting out of, 94; fitting of, 90; layout for napped skins, 91; layout of, 90–91; piecing of, 87; preparation of, 90; use of on patterned skins, 91

Pickling, 10

Piecing, 110

Pigsuede, washing of, 117

Piping, 77–78; corded, 77–78

Plating, 13

Pockets: facings for, 104–105; flaps for, 72; templates for, 70; welt, 70

Pressing methods, 35; for construction details, 35

Pressing equipment: mallet, 29; marble slab, 29; seam stick, 29

Prickstitch, 69

Projects: belts, 45–47; caps, 60–62; hats, 60–62; purses, 53–59; unlined vests, 49–52

Purses, 53–59; linings for, 53, 58

Quilting, 110-111; batting for, 110 111

Retanning, 11; mineral agents for, 12

Seam tapes, 66

Seams: bound, 81; curved, finishing of, 33; double topstitched plain, 38; flat-felled, 39; for suede, 36–37; for leather, 36-37; lapped, 41–42; mock welt, 36, 40; plain, 36; slot, 42; thick, dealing with, 34; topstitched plain, 38

Related Titles
from Lark Books

Index, *continued*

Setting out, 12

Sewing machine accessories: roller foot, 25; walking foot, 25;

Sewing machine needles: choosing, 32; jeans needles, 26; leather needles, 26; stretch needles, 26; universal point, 26

Side leather, 11

Skins: defined, 15; size chart, 21; size of, 21; storage of, 117

Skirt linings, 95–97

Snaps, 84

Sorting, 11

Spewing, 20

Split, 11

Splitting, 11

Stain removal, 118

Staking, 12

Stamping, 113; paints for, 113

Stenciling, 113; paints for, 113

Stitch length, 32

Stitching, directional, 33

Suede: defined, 16; home cleaning of, 119; removing marks from, 35; washing of, 117

Synthetic tanning agents, 11

Tanning: brain, 9, chrome, 10, vegetable, 9

Tanning process, 9–14

Teflon foot, 25, 32

Thread: bonded nylon, 27; cotton-wrapped polyester, 27; for topstitching, 27; long-staple polyester, 27

Topstitching, 36

Underlinings, 66

Unhairing, 10

Vegetable extracts, 11

Vest linings, 99-100

Vests, unlined, 49-52

Waistbands, 75–77; faced, 76; hanger loops in, 75; tailored, 75–76

Waistlines, faced, 76–77

Waists: elastic, 77; for heavy leather, 77;

Weaving, 112

Wetting back, 12

Wringing, 11

Wrinkle removal, 118

Yardage equivalents, 21; conversion chart for, 21

Zippers, 69–70